JESUS IS
MY UNCLE

JESUS IS MY UNCLE

Christology from a Hispanic Perspective

Luis G. Pedraja

Abingdon Press
Nashville

JESUS IS MY UNCLE: CHRISTOLOGY FROM A HISPANIC PERSPECTIVE

This book is printed on recycled, acid-free, elemental-chlorine–free paper.

Library of Congress Cataloging-in-Publication Data

Pedraja, Luis G., 1963–
    Jesus is my uncle : Christology from a Hispanic perspective / Luis G. Pedraja.
       p   cm.
    Includes bibliographical references.
    ISBN 0-687-05996-8 (alk. paper)
    1. Jesus Christ—Person and offices.   2. Hispanic American theology.   I. Title.
    BT202.P395   1999
    232'.089'68—dc21   99-10158
                                                                                          CIP

Scripture quotations, unless otherwise indicated, are from the New Revised Standard Version Bible, copyright © 1989, by the Division of Christian Education of the National Council of the Churches of Christ in the United States of America.

99 00 01 02 03 04 05 06 07 08—10 9 8 7 6 5 4 3 2 1

MANUFACTURED IN THE UNITED STATES OF AMERICA

To
my wife, who believed in me,
my family, who inspired me,
and, of course, to my uncle Jesús

— CONTENTS —

Acknowledgments 9

Foreword 11

1. What's in a Name? 15

2. Jesus Loves Me 39

3. And the Verb Became Flesh 60

4. God Is a Verb 85

5. Love Enacted 107

Notes 125

Bibliography 138

─ ACKNOWLEDGMENTS ─

When I began writing this book, I did not set out to write a Christology. My original intentions were to write a theological piece on the Trinity, language, and its significance for Hispanic theology. However, two things happened that changed my mind. First, right from the onset, I realized that it was impossible to write about the Trinity without contending with the person and work of Christ. To speak about the Trinity one must already have a Christology, even if it is just implied. Second, while lecturing on Christology to my systematic theology class at Perkins School of Theology, I began to unpack the christological implications of language and of thinking about Jesus as God's Verb. As a result, my thoughts and my writing turned to the topic of Christology.

Through the writing of this book, I also came to realize the value and significance of doing Hispanic theology as a community. Although I had worked in other projects and anthologies that developed as a collaborative enterprise within our Hispanic theological community, as well as in dialogue with our churches, this was my first time authoring a book. I quickly discovered the graciousness of many friends and colleagues who willingly gave of their time in reading my manuscripts and offering suggestions. At the same time, I discovered how much I relied on my experiences within the Hispanic communities and churches throughout my life.

I will always be grateful to Justo González for his encouragement, mentoring, and guidance. I am also grateful for the support of the Hispanic Theological Initiative, its director, Daisy Machado, and Pew Charitable Trust for the postdoctoral grant that allowed me to take a full-year sabbatical to finish my book. I am also grateful to Dean Robin Lovin, David Maldonado, Perkins School of Theology, and Southern Methodist University for allowing me to have a year's research leave and for supplementing the funds provided by the Hispanic Theological Initiative.

It is impossible to name all of my friends and colleagues who offered encouragement, support, and suggestions during the time that I spent writing this book. I am especially grateful to Ada Maria Isasi-Diaz, Ismael García, and Charles Wood, who all read portions of my manuscript and offered many helpful suggestions. I am also grateful for those students and colleagues at Perkins School of Theology whose constant encouragement and feedback kept me motivated and focused. Also, the invaluable help of my research assistants, Donna Yarri and Kimberly Neve, is greatly appreciated. It is hard to imagine how I could have accomplished the tasks involved in writing this book without their assistance.

Finally, I would be remiss if I did not express my gratitude to my wife, Amber, whose patience, encouragement, and support kept me motivated. If it had not been for her constant friendly reminders that I had a book to write, it would have been impossible to meet my deadlines in a timely manner. Her encouragement, along with that of our extended families, was a breath of fresh air during those lonely hours spent in my office awaiting some form of divine inspiration, or at least some sort of inspiration! And of course, my eternal gratitude to Jesus, without whom there would be no Christology at all, and to my uncle Jesús, whose name made the search for a title much easier.

Luis G. Pedraja
Dallas, Texas

— FOREWORD —

When Jesus came into the district of Caesarea Philippi, he asked his disciples, "Who do people say that the Son of Man is?" From the disciples' answer, we gather that there was quite a variety of opinions. Simon the fisherman, as usual, topped them all: "You are the Messiah, the Son of the living God." Ever since, that has been one of the standard answers that Christians and the church have given to the question, "Who is Jesus?"

That answer may be correct, but it is not the whole answer. Indeed, throughout the ages Christians, while agreeing that Jesus is the Messiah, the Son of the living God, have understood this in many different ways: he is the sacrificial victim for our sins; he is the great example of love and virtue; he is the conqueror of the powers of evil; he is the great teacher of wisdom; he is the suffering servant as well as the king of heaven; he is the Lion of Judah and also the Lamb that was slain.

All of these answers are correct. They each add something to our knowledge and understanding of Jesus. Something would be lost were we to see him only as the king of heaven, and not as the suffering servant. Indeed, more than just something is lost when we insist that our answer is complete, final, absolutely correct. What is lost is the sovereign otherness of Jesus, who will not be confined to our narrow definitions or our fixed orthodoxy.

That is not to say that Jesus is like a mirror in which we see ourselves. Jesus is indeed another, one whom we must come to know as another, not as a mere projection of what we wish life would be. Yet precisely because he is not us, because he is another, he relates to each of us according to who we are. Thus, Simon the fisherman from Galilee saw in him the fulfillment of all the aspirations of the Jewish people, the Anointed One; Christians oppressed by their own sin and by societal sin saw him as the conqueror of the powers of evil; the medieval monk who knew that all his monastic discipline would never come close to atoning for his sin saw in him the victim that paid in his stead. Jesus is all of this and much more; and we discover some of what that "much more" may be as we listen to what others, out of their own experience and perspective, have come to see in him.

Luis Pedraja had an uncle whose name was Jesús. This provides him for the opening line of the book, but that is not all. Even today, as a carefully trained and sophisticated theologian, Pedraja remains the one whose uncle was Jesús. It is thus that culture and tradition function. They are not items one can put on and off, like a jacket. They are part of one's very being and perspective. We may deny them, but they are still there. We may accept a theology that was forged in a different culture and situation; but our life and our actual faith will remain dissonant with that theology.

This is why what Dr. Pedraja says about language in the pages that follow is significant. We employ language as a basic tool of thought and of communication. When languages have different structures, the structure of thought also varies. When we speak the same truth—in this case the name of Jesus—in another language, we discover in it dimensions we had not suspected.

Therefore, what is important in this book is not that Pedraja had an uncle whose name was Jesús, nor that the etymology of *incarnation* comes across much more clearly in Spanish, nor that Pedraja grew up reading *logos* as *Verbo*. All of these are important parts of his argument; but none of it is as important as the main thrust of this book, namely that when we look at Jesus through different cultural eyes, our image of Jesus is enriched. For those of us who, like Pedraja, grew up with uncles and neighbors whose name was Jesús, and who bought *carne* in the *carnicería*, this book will bring theology and piety to a greater accord. For those readers who never knew anyone named Jesus, and who might even be scandalized at the thought, this book will bring the Jesus of their devotion closer to their life-experience. The purpose of this book, as I read Pedraja's intent, is that all of us attain a fuller understanding of Jesus, and that by understanding him better we may also be able to follow him more closely because we are also closer to each other.

What all of this means, succinctly stated, is that this is a book about Christology. It is not about the Spanish language—even though it says much about that language. It is not a book about Hispanic Christology—even though what it presents is a Hispanic Christology. It is a book about Christology. It is a book about Christ. It is a book that should enrich our response to the age-old question: "Who do you say I am?"

Justo L. González
Decatur, Georgia
October 4, 1998 (Day of the Feast of St. Francis)

— 1 —
WHAT'S IN A NAME?

Jesus is my uncle. He also was my next-door neighbor, a boy in my school, and a deacon in my church. Jesus is not just the name of God's Son, it is also the name of many of my friends, relatives, and neighbors in the Hispanic community. When well-meaning missionaries periodically came by the house to ask us if we knew Jesus, they were surprised when we would answer, "Yes, he lives in that house across the street." Unlike my English-speaking friends who considered it sacrilegious to name someone after God's Son, Hispanics consider it an honor and a constant reminder of God's nearness. Eventually, as some of my relatives and friends became *evangélicos* (Protestants) or entered the English-speaking world, they changed their names from Jesus to less sacrilegious names to conform to the norms of churches and individuals influenced by the values of an English-speaking world. That is why my uncle is no longer Jesús. He calls himself Carlos. And the deacon in my old church is now Josué.

Nevertheless, I grew up thinking of God's Son as someone who lived near me and who had a human face like those who bore his name. He was close to me and concretely present in my life. Just like my neighbors, relatives, and friends, Jesus also lived in our community. He was someone we could call upon to understand our plight and to give us hope. The name of Jesus was not taboo. It was not a name reserved for some faraway deity whom we risked offending. Instead, it was a name that we could call upon at any time, and we would call upon that name often. Calling Jesus' name out loud when we heard bad news or came close to having an accident was not a curse or a sacrilege as it was for my friends from the United States. It was an exclamatory prayer spoken in despair, fear, or surprise. It was a good thing. It was even a blessing we would say when someone sneezed, much as people say "bless you" in English.

My culture, experience, and language affected my perceptions of religion. The way we talked and thought about Jesus in Spanish felt qualitatively different for me than what I experienced in English-speaking congregations. Jesus felt closer and more real to me in Spanish. As a Latina woman in a congregation once told me: "When I worship God in English it does not feel like I am really worshiping God, but when I worship God in Spanish, I feel satisfied."

READING THEOLOGY IN SPANISH

Our language and our culture affect the way we perceive God; therefore they have an important effect upon our theological formation.[1] Through them, our theological perspectives and perceptions can change drastically. Our language and culture can enrich our theology and our faith, but they can also cause limitations and biases. Unless we pay closer attention to these influences, our theology will suffer as a result.

With the rapid growth of Hispanic communities in the United States, it is imperative that churches, pastors, and theologians become aware of the roles language and culture play in their work. Such an awareness can enhance their theological insights and facilitate their work with these growing communities. As we become more aware of different theological insights, we are better able to understand one another and God. Rather than adding to the dissonance of clashing voices or the tedious monotony of a singular voice that drowns out all others, we can expand our theology into a melody of complementary voices and harmonies. By promoting dialogue and heightening awareness among ourselves, we can gain new theological insights and uncover our own biases and distortions. This process benefits everyone by dissolving many rigid cultural paradigms and increasing our mutual understanding, while appreciating the richness and value of our respective traditions.

The experience of Hispanics in the United States has created a new sense of culture and language defined by at least two cultures and two languages, creating a new perspective defined by bilingualism and biculturalism.[2] By doing theology through bicultural and bilingual lenses, our theological vision becomes broader and sharper. Through these lenses we can see how our language and culture affect and influence our theology and our perspectives. In turn, these insights expand our perspectives and theological insights. As a Hispanic American, I inhabit both worlds. Thus, I can see the beauty and danger both worlds offer to theology, and why it is important to take our culture and language seriously. Through this book, I will share my bilingual and bicultural lenses with you so that you can see better how they affect Christology and offer new insights into Christian theology.

In sharing these particular insights, I do not profess to speak for all Hispanics. No one can ever hope to capture the vast differences embodied by all the individuals who participate in any given culture. Nor can anyone profess to speak for everyone who shares his or her culture. In the case of Hispanics the task is even more daunting, for the term *Hispanic* glosses over a vast array of cultures, nationalities, and races that share at least a partial cultural and linguistic heritage.

Thus, it is not my intent to become the self-appointed spokesman for Hispanics. All I can offer is a sketch of the Hispanic reality from my perspective, that of a Cuban-American Protestant theologian who was born into the Catholic Church and who has served as pastor to many different Hispanic parishioners. As a result, this sketch, like many others, often glosses over the broad diversity of experiences contained within the Hispanic community while highlighting some of our shared traits and struggles. When I speak of Hispanics, I am speaking of those communities in which I have had the privilege to participate. I am speaking of the Cuban-American neighborhoods of Little Havana in Miami where I grew up, of the Baptist churches I attended, of the Mexican migrant workers in central Florida whom I pastored, and of the many other groups of Hispanics to whom I ministered. When I speak of Hispanics, I am not referring to an abstract whole. Rather, I am referring to flesh-and-blood individuals.

Hispanic theologians take seriously the experiences of the many diverse individuals who form our community. They also take culture seriously as they reflect on the experiences, practices, and faiths of Hispanic communities in the United States. Consequently, they interpret the theological content of Hispanic culture, provide a vision of hope for the future, and offer a direction for action in the present. Through ethnographic analysis and the study of culture, Hispanic theologians describe the theological content of the people's faith and prescribe ways to change oppressive conditions. In addition, they provide new theological insights and an increased awareness of the role culture plays in the development of faith and theology. Thus, their contributions to theology should not be ignored or minimized.

Some Hispanic theologians believe that theological reflection should begin with human experience. This does not mean that they deny other sources for doing theology; rather, it means that what we experience in our lives, families, cultures, communities, and practices shapes our understanding of our faith. Experience is the medium through which our theology is acquired, shaped, and transmitted.[3] Even the Bible we read and the community in which we worship contribute to these experiences that shape us and our culture. As culture shapes us, we too contribute our unique insights and characteristics to it, adding to the whole body of culture for generations to come. Hispanic theologians also believe that theology must be ready to discern when, where, and how God is active within these cultural contexts. As a result, theology must be attentive to the cultures, struggles, and communities of faith in which it participates.

Justo González, in his book *Mañana: Christian Theology from a Hispanic Perspective,* challenges us to read the Bible "in Spanish." He does not mean that everyone should learn the Spanish language. What he wants us to do is to thoughtfully consider the challenges and perspectives that Hispanics bring to the biblical text.[4] This "reading" requires us to look at the text with a certain hermeneutic of suspicion that considers the effects of power and sociopolitical structures. González's "grammar" for reading the Bible in Spanish calls us to take seriously the experiences and readings of those who are the "little ones of our society." It challenges us to look at how the poor, the oppressed, the marginalized, and the alienated read the Scriptures.[5] But it also carries an emphasis on the way in which we use language. According to González, the Bible was originally meant to be read both in the vocative and in community. In other words, the Bible addresses us and forces us to confront *its* "reading" of *us.*

Nor is our reading of the Bible a private enterprise. It is a public affair that affects the community as a whole and is carried out by the community as a whole.[6] The Scriptures are a product of particular communities and languages, and they are transmitted through particular communities and languages. These cultures and languages are not passive recipients of the Scriptures; they help mold them and in turn are also molded by them. The Bible shapes us and our community of faith.

Hispanic theologians challenge us to do theology in a Hispanic context and to see theology from a Hispanic perspective. These tasks require us to go beyond reading the Bible in Spanish to reading our theology in Spanish. As with the Bible, reading theology in Spanish does not call us to learn the Spanish language. Instead, it challenges us to reexamine the way we do theology and to reformulate it to include the perspectives of the Hispanic community, taking seriously this community's experiences and theological interpretations. Doing theology in Spanish also requires us to examine the socioeconomic, cultural, linguistic, and political issues that shape our theology.

Reading theology in Spanish means that we must be attentive to the struggles and marginalization encountered by Hispanics in the United States. For Hispanics, even the way we speak and look has been a source of marginalization. Regardless of our differences, most Hispanics in the United States generally face oppression at one level or another: prejudice, ridicule, and alienation because of our accent, race, and culture. I have been ridiculed at a Christian college because of my name, considered a criminal suspect while at seminary because of my accent, and even confronted by a major department store's security after complaining about an incorrect price tag on a shirt! Yet these experiences are not unique. Most Hispanics I know could tell similar stories of discrimination and bias.

The majority of Hispanics are familiar with poverty, either personally or in the recent history of their families and friends. For some, their limited use of English or their limited schooling often curtails their hopes for socioeconomic advancement. This does not mean that they are uneducated or that they desire no education. They just lack the luxury of time to spend obtaining a proper education at school. As teenagers they often are called upon to work so that they can help support their families, limiting the time they can dedicate to their studies. Many of them are barely able to finish their high school education. With the rising costs of higher education and an almost unbearable demand on their time, they are often unable to make the grades or to afford a college degree.

Like many other minorities, many Hispanics struggle against discrimination at work, school, and church. Even the few and fortunate Hispanics who have obtained an education or have amassed some wealth still face discrimination and pressures to conform to the cultural standards of those in power. When we consider the experiences of most Hispanics from a theological perspective, it makes sense that most Hispanic theologians demand action and social change. Thus, a proper reading of theology in Spanish should provide ways for empowerment, liberation, and restoration.

Another aspect of reading theology in Spanish is an awareness of how culture affects theology. The multicultural nature of Hispanic theologies also allows us to gain a broader theological perspective—a perspective that enriches the entire Christian community. By incorporating some of the imagery and insights that come from different cultures and religious traditions, Hispanic theologians create new vehicles for understanding and expressing the Christian faith. This aspect is evident in one of the principal areas of reflection for Hispanic theologians: popular religion.

In this context, popular religion does not mean those aspects of religion that are in fashion or popular in society at large. Rather, popular religion refers to those rites and practices that express and exemplify the faith of the people in ways that are not always part of official church celebrations. Generally, these practices are innovations upon the accepted rituals of the church that add elements of native cultures and express the people's faith, hopes, and quest for self-expression through concrete symbols and forms.[7] As a result, these innovative rituals empower the people to express their own identity while resisting liturgical impositions from the church. Through popular religion the faith and culture of the Hispanic people become incarnate in their religious practices and symbols. These rituals and practices of popular religion provide a rich source of images and symbols that aesthetically express dimensions of our faith for which words fail. Popular religion itself is a bridge between different cultures and religious traditions that enables Hispanic Christianity to express itself through new vehicles, images, and constructs.

Popular religion has a different form within Hispanic Protestant traditions than within Hispanic Catholic traditions. The iconoclastic tendencies of Protestants force them to reject the concrete symbols and imagery that often prevail in Catholicism. As a result, Hispanic Protestant popular religion becomes more centered around the spoken and written word. Innovations occur in the use of festive music, testimonies, and prayers. Hispanic Protestant mainline churches transcend their denominational boundaries and incorporate aspects of Pentecostal traditions into their worship that provide more festive expressions of Hispanic culture through music and overt self-expression such as clapping, shouting, and the sharing of personal experiences. Such practices as *testimonios* (testimonies) allow laypeople to share their faith, struggles, and hopes within the structure of the worship service. Prayer meetings and Bible studies also allow people to express themselves and to gain empowerment through their self-expression and communal support. As a result, language becomes a vehicle for empowerment in popular religion within these congregations.[8]

Language also plays an important role in the Hispanic experience. The diversity found in the Hispanic communities of the United States is astounding. We Hispanics are as diverse in the food we eat as we are diverse in our cultures, nationalities, religions, and appearance. However, in spite of our diversity, we share some common struggles, hopes, and qualities. Through the ongoing dialogue between Hispanic theologians and our communities, we are slowly finding common ground and a sense of unity while affirming our diversity as a source of strength.

Among the things we share, most of us have a common heritage in the Spanish language, making it a vital part of our identity as Hispanics.[9] Since language is the medium for expressing and interpreting experiences, I want to challenge us to look not only at experience and culture but also at the role language plays in our theology. In a sense, I want to challenge us to learn to read theology in Spanish not just in the context of experience but also in a more literal sense: to examine our theological language and the contributions that language can make to our theological thinking. The power of language for the Hispanic community is central to its cultural identity and to its sociotheological construction, as well as to the preservation of its heritage.[10]

Yet doing and reading theology in Spanish is not something

limited to the Hispanic communities. The perspectives that Hispanic Americans bring to theology help broaden everyone's horizons and enrich everyone's understanding of God. One of the salient characteristics of Hispanic theologies is a growing propensity to doing theology in dialogue with others.[11] Hispanic theologians often do theology in community and in dialogue.[12] This dialogue ultimately should be an ongoing broadening of our theology into a cooperative enterprise in which we share our limited individual perspectives of an infinite God with each other. Since no single human perspective with all its limitations can ever hope to contain the full reality of God, theology must be open to growth and to dialogue.

Finally, reading theology in Spanish also requires that we examine how our cultural perspectives and our language can contribute new theological insights. Our different standpoints provide us with different ways of envisioning both God and ourselves. Our different perspectives are similar to a broad landscape viewed from different places. While each person might be looking at the same scenery, each will see different aspects of it depending upon his or her angle, interests, and standpoint. Others might even be able to see our place in the landscape better than we can![13]

The same illustration can be applied to our theology. Often we notice only the things about God that interest us and that are in our best interest. Seldom can we see our location, interests, motives, and relationship to God as clearly as we think we do. In sharing our perspectives with each other, we avoid the distortions of our narrow viewpoint and enhance both our understanding and our appreciation of God.[14] As we listen to each other, we are challenged to broaden our theology to be more inclusive. Thus, we are able to contribute to other people's understanding of God while we also grow in our own. As we examine the imagery, affections, and perspectives of Hispanic culture, experience, and language, we can enhance the way we think about God and the way we do theology.

LANGUAGE AND THEOLOGY

Beyond the immediacy of experience and action, theology is primarily a linguistic enterprise.[15] Unlike some other academic disciplines, theology uses language as its primary tool. This means that, at least at some points in their life, everyone is a theologian. When we read the Bible we are doing theology. When we share our faith we are doing theology. Whenever we speak about God, we are doing theology. However, theology is more than just "talk about God." The Greek word *logos* is far richer in meaning than our English translation of it as "word." It can also mean "reason," "reckoning," "motive," "command," and even a "creative word."[16] Doing theology as an academic enterprise involves thinking about God and our faith. It requires that we give a "reason" for our faith, which requires us to examine and to think critically about our faith.

However, theology can be more than just a cognitive enterprise. It can be a way of communing with God and communicating our experience of God to others. Doing theology can become a way of life. The cognitive, affective, and practical aspects of theology cannot be tidily separated from each other. Likewise our faith, words, and deeds cannot be severed from our theology.

Language plays an important role in our theology and in our community. We communicate through language, and in the act of communicating we come to know ourselves, enter into relationships, and create communities. Depending on its context, the word *relate* itself can mean both telling a story and being in a relationship. Our ability to speak, write, gesture, act, and share with one another creates a communion between ourselves and others. Relating (telling) a story or event in our life fosters relationships with others and empowers them to "relate" to us and to those who are in relationships with us. In this fostering of relationship we find the inherent power of sharing our faith with others. Our telling to others of our faith empowers them to enter into a faith relationship with God.

Since language is so essential to our community, faith, and theological enterprise, we should explore how it affects these elements of our lives. However, in examining our theology in this manner, we could easily become entangled in a linguistic study of etymologies or fall prey to a comparative study of languages that sets one language against the other. But instead of a linguistic study of theology, I propose that we look at how certain terms and uses of language can enhance our understanding of theology and theological language.

This examination of language explores how our experiences and linguistic expressions enhance our theological perspectives by creating new ways of envisioning God. Such an exercise can be done in most cultures and languages. However, I am a Hispanic. I grew up thinking in Spanish and immersed in Hispanic culture. I read the Bible in Spanish and prayed in Spanish. I knew people named Jesus. Through my native language I was able to commune with God and live in a community of faith. Therefore, it is natural for me to look at how my particular culture and language can influence theology. Since our language reflects and affects the way we envision God's interaction with humanity, Hispanic theologians must examine the language that mediates the experiences and faith of the Hispanic community. We must not only learn to read theology in Spanish by examining Hispanic culture, but also learn to read how our language can affect theology and enhance our theological imagery.

EXPERIENCE, LANGUAGE, AND HISPANIC THEOLOGY

In a recent conversation I had with the noted philosopher and theologian Charles Hartshorne, he made a telling remark regarding the significance of language. In the context of our conversation about the "spin" that people place on words to favor their arguments, he said: "If you have no respect for language, you have no respect for those who use the language."[17] Our language is so intricately related to our culture, experiences, and identity that it is essential that we give it due consideration in our theological reflection.[18]

Our language is an integral part of our spirituality that both reflects and affects our theology. The affections, nuances, and conceptual weight of the words we use can influence our theology. For instance, the contemporary use of inclusive language recognizes the important role language plays in our theological formation; the gender we use in referring to God not only reflects certain preconceptions and biases but also affects the way we envision divine attributes such as power and compassion.[19]

Furthermore, the way we use language is also telling of the power structures of a society, since those who control the power also tend to define what is normative in language. As a result, marginalized groups and theologies carry qualifiers, such as "Hispanic" theology, while those who are in power simply see their theologies and experiences as universal and thus as the normative or universal expression of theology.[20]

Language is also affective and rich with images, associations, and connotations that transcend its cognitive dimensions.[21] In the same manner that language can shape our experiences, our experiences can shape our language. For instance, when we hear the word *mom* or *dad* our thoughts are not limited to a cognitive experience of an abstract or generic "mother" or "father." Instead, we associate the words with concrete images of our own mother and our own father, as well as with all the related experiences and feelings attached to them. Depending upon the nature of our past experiences and family life, we attach positive or negative emotions to these words. As a result, they can evoke, for example, feelings of security and nurture or feelings of fear and sorrow. Our language is pregnant with extralinguistic images, feelings, and memories that enhance the meaning and significance of our words and phrases beyond the merely cognitive sphere. These images, feelings, and memories can affect the way we view reality and think about God.

Similarly, we think of other words and meanings as linked to another word. These connections give a particular word a different "feel" from other words that lack similar connections. Ludwig Wittgenstein, an early-twentieth-century philosopher, argued that language is a framework of words held together by other words.[22] This image compares language to a building being constructed. Some words are so basic that they serve as the foundation for the whole structure of language. We cannot function without them. Also, it makes no sense to ask what those words mean since they are so basic that we take their meaning for granted.[23] We know how to use them correctly, but their definition always eludes us. Words such as the verb "to be," conjunctions (and, but), and demonstrative pronouns (this, that) are very difficult to define, yet we always know how to use them.[24]

Some words acquire their meanings by the way they are used in connection with other words. The ways in which these words come together create different meanings and nuances. For example, the word *lamb* means something different when we use it in church than when we use it at a restaurant. In some instances, different usages of the same word enrich its nuances. For example, the Spanish word *pastor* is ordinarily used for both a "shepherd" and a "minister," further enriching the notion of a minister serving as a shepherd to his or her "flock." Although English uses *pastor* to refer to a minister, it does not immediately invoke the same kind of imageries and associations that it does in Spanish. However, the association of "congregation" with "flock" in English clearly invokes the image of the pastor as a "shepherd."

According to Wittgenstein, language is like a game. We do not connect words directly to things we see. Instead, we learn the "rules" of the game by seeing how others use words within a particular language.[25] In the same manner in which we learn the rules for moving a pawn in chess, we learn the rules for proper word use within the frameworks of a given language and context.[26] For instance, I know that the words *lamb* and *shepherd* mean something different when I use them in church than when I use them at a restaurant or on a farm. When I speak Spanish or English, I know the way certain words should be used. For instance, I know when we should use *ser* and when we should use *estar,* the two forms of the verb "to be" in Spanish. I know that the former is more permanent and essential to a particular state of being than the latter. However, when someone asks me why one should use one rather than the other in a given instance, I am not always able to give a good reason. I just know the way it works. Similarly, I can tell you whether a given noun or object in Spanish is grammatically feminine or masculine. I can tell you that the chair *(la silla)* is feminine and carries a feminine article. I can also tell you that the couch *(el sofá)* is masculine and carries a masculine article. But I cannot tell you why I know that an (asexual) inanimate object belongs to a particular grammatical gender in Spanish. I just know that is the way these words are used.

More recently, postmodern philosophers such as Jacques Derrida have argued that words do not necessarily acquire meaning by their correlation to objects in the world. Instead, words acquire meaning through their interplay with other words in the language.[27] As a result, the context of the words in a language and the interpretations of these words by the readers also affect their meaning. Thus, Derrida argues that the meanings of words are not necessarily fixed by an objective referent or correlation to reality. Instead they are fluid, contextual, and open to interpretation.

While I do not agree completely with Derrida's relativism—I believe the meaning of words does have some correlation to the world we inhabit—I do agree that there is a certain fluidity and openness to the meaning of many words that varies due to their linguistic context. While words have a referent outside of language, they are not fixed in their definitions and meaning by a dictionary or even by their reference. Words acquire meaning through their context and through their use. Thus, our context, whether it is textual, linguistic, or cultural, affects the meaning of the words we use. In other words, the truth might be out there, as a currently popular television show advocates, but it is always conditioned by our own perspectives, biases, and contexts.

Our syntax, the way we put words together, and the context of our writing can change the meanings of the words we use. We can create new meanings by using words in unusual contrasts and contexts that enhance their meanings and create new images. If I say "God's voice is like a roaring lion," the words evoke a certain image in your mind. You can envision the power and fear that a lion's roar conveys. But if I say "God's voice is like a silent roar," it creates a completely new image of reality that we might have never conceived. In placing together two usually contradictory words, we create an entirely new meaning and vision of what God's voice is like, one that at first throws our preconceptions for a loop.

Finally, our own personal context also affects the meanings we attach to words. For example, the same words used in different settings can have entirely different meanings. Alfred North Whitehead, an early-twentieth-century British philosopher, illustrated this difference in one of his lectures with the phrase "a warm summer day." The phrase means entirely different things for someone living in Texas and for someone living in northern Britain.[28] A warm summer day in Texas is not as pleasant and temperate as it would be in northern Britain. Even time changes the meaning, perception, and images we associate with certain words. When we use the words *universe* or *earth* they convey far different images to us in the twentieth century than they conveyed to people living in the early Middle Ages, who envisioned a firmament above and a flat world at the center of the universe under their feet.

THE LANGUAGE OF FAITH

Biblical scholars know the importance that language, context, culture, and location play in interpreting the biblical texts. Their exegesis of a text allows them to form a richer understanding of a passage by elucidating its nuances, cultural significance, and the poetic overtones that could easily be missed in a translation. Similarly, our own theological language is also laden with feelings and imagery that often go unnoticed.

Most scholars know that regardless of how well they know a biblical language, they will never understand the nuances of the language like a native speaker.[29] This statement is also true about the languages we use to express our theology and our faith. Nonnative speakers often miss the nuances and images a language conveys. These subtleties can even be taken for granted by native speakers, who fail to recognize them consciously. Left unexamined, these words create images and concepts that surreptitiously affect and shape our theological thinking.

Our experiences also shape and color the way we use language. The nearness of God I felt as a child is reflected in the way I speak about God; because we felt the nearness of Jesus to our community, we also spoke of Jesus as someone who was near. Thus, children were named after Jesus and people would call out the name of Jesus prayerfully when in need. The sense of intimacy, solidarity, and nearness our community of faith felt with Jesus allowed us to call upon his name with ease and love. Some even used *"Jesusito," "Chuy,"* and other diminutives of endearment for Jesus that are not heard in English.[30] We identified with Jesus because we felt that he knew what it was like to hope, love, suffer, and die. In short, we felt that he knew what it was like to be human, poor, and powerless. Jesus knew what it was like to be one of us.

Growing up, we spoke Spanish at home and at church. We even thought in Spanish. When we read the Scriptures, we read them in Spanish. We sang and prayed in Spanish—and God understood us. Our experiences shaped our language, and our language shaped how we understood God and how we expressed ourselves to God. Within our church community, we shared our feelings, our faith, and our hopes, further loading our language with the emotions and images we associated with our community of faith. When these words were translated into English or into another language, they no longer carried the same intensity and memories that they did in Spanish. It was no longer the same language we associated with our faith.

The role language plays in our theology and in our faith is not a role unique to Spanish. All languages become laden with emotions, images, and experiences that its speakers associate with their faith and with their community.[31] Just like the Latina woman who did not feel satisfied worshiping in English, many English speakers feel satisfied only when they use the King James version of the Bible in their worship. Although they might not understand some of the words and might find it difficult to read, they resist attempts to use a more contemporary translation of the Bible. For these people, the language of the King James Bible is the language that carries the affections of their faith. Like Spanish for the Latina woman, its language is their language of faith. Without it, they do not feel as though they are worshiping God.

THE LIMITS OF THEOLOGICAL LANGUAGE

All languages impose certain limitations upon us. Just as some words can open up new ways for understanding reality, others can conceal reality or leave us without response. Just as our experiences can affect our language, so our words can define our experiences. But definitions also confine. Both *define* and *confine* carry the Latin root *finis*, which means "end" or "limits." Words create a boundary around the fluidity of our experience, allowing us to abstract only certain aspects of our experience. This process of abstraction is one of the strengths of language. Language allows us to manipulate and organize these abstract aspects of our experience. As we create different connections between these abstractions, we can expand the horizons of our understanding beyond the immediate experience of our environment. Thus, we can envision fictional worlds, unactualized possibilities, and alternate constructions of our past. We also can systematize our experiences by placing them in orderly categories, or we can even explore their different patterns.

However, these abstractions also confine our experience to static categories, creating distortions in our interpretations. Studies show that people have more difficulty recognizing nonverbal experiences such as images, smells, and tastes when they try to remember them through verbal descriptions, because nonverbal perceptions are not always easily reducible to verbal descriptions.[32] This is also the case in religion, where experiences that transcend our linguistic capabilities are remembered through rituals, imagery, and symbolism that cannot always be reduced to the linguistic abstractions that predominate in theology. If we forget the limitations of language and confuse our linguistic abstractions with reality, we limit our understanding to a very narrow perspective.[33] And if we impose this narrow perspective on others, we become oppressors and impoverish ourselves of the richness of diverse perspectives.

When our language refers to God, the limits of language become even more pronounced. Throughout the first volume of his *Church Dogmatics*, Karl Barth continually emphasized the difficulties inherent in our language about God. According to him, the broken and limited nature of our languages can never fully express the reality of God.[34] These limitations prevent us from fully grasping God within the inherent confines of human language. Virgilio Elizondo, a Mexican-American theologian, writes that the native Nahuatl theologians of Mexico also believed that human language was insufficient for speaking about the divine. As a result, divine truth could only be expressed through flowers (images of beauty) and song (poetic melody). They alone could transcend rational discourse and empower the imagination, allowing human beings to engage the divine.[35] The Nahuatl theologians understood something we sometimes forget: theological language must often resort to imagery, aesthetics, and metaphor to express the divine.

Whenever we encounter God, we try to make sense of what has occurred. We extrapolate certain characteristics from these encounters, from philosophical reflections, and from other aspects of our experience. In other words, we abstract aspects of our experience and correlate them with other experiences to develop a notion of God. We then attribute these notions to God. Since we use language to interpret and convey our experiences, these experiences become limited by the words and expressions available to our language, as well as by the context of our language.

Although the limitations of our languages affect our theology, they do not necessarily prevent us from engaging in the task of doing theology. According to Barth, we are able to speak about

God because God "sanctifies" our language to enable it to bear witness of God to us.[36] Just as we are justified in spite of our fallen nature, our language is justified and used in spite of its limitations. In other words, God speaks to our situations in ways that are meaningful to us at a level we can understand.

Paul Tillich, another twentieth-century theologian, argued that God speaks to us in concrete and specific ways that address our particular circumstances and contexts as a person or group.[37] God addresses us through the concrete and limited vehicles of our languages and experiences. Our immediate experience of God is intrinsically connected to our situation, culture, and history. Whenever we encounter God, it is in concrete situations and contexts. Just as at Pentecost, God speaks to us in our own tongues in spite of their limitations (Acts 2:4-6).

Beyond our immediate experience of God, our knowledge of God is primarily interpreted through our cultural and cognitive contexts and conveyed within the confines of human language. All of these factors color and shape our theology.[38] As a result, we need to become aware of their effect on our theology. Both languages and theologies are living realities that grow and change like the people who embody them. When our theological language becomes fixed in archaic constructs, it risks losing its relevance to society and even to ourselves. The dynamic nature of language forces us to continually rethink our theology, preventing it from becoming "fossilized in final form."[39] In addition, a good theology must speak beyond the closed academic circles of universities and scholars and speak the language of the people and empower their faith.

THE PARADOX OF TRANSLATION

Language has an inherent power to create images and evoke feelings that can shape the way we envision reality, including God. When we translate words and phrases from one language to another, we risk losing those images and feelings. The word *translate* comes from the Latin word *translatus,* a form of the Latin verb *transfero,* meaning "to carry over" or "to transfer." When we translate a word, we "carry" or "transfer" its meaning into another language. However, this does not mean that the words themselves are identical in their nuances and imagery. It only means that they are used in similar ways.

In Spanish, the word we currently use for "translating" is *tra-ducir*.[40] This is a word with an interesting background. It comes from the Latin word *traduco*, meaning "to transfer or transport," and carries the connotation of moving from one context into another. Like the word *translation*, it has the prefix *trans*, which means "to move over," together with *duco*, which means "to lead or escort." These are the same words from which we get English words such as *transportation* (to carry over) and conduct (to lead with). In the act of translation we are in effect leading words from one context into another.

The act of translation is a paradoxical venture. We affirm that it can be done, but we must affirm also that we face limitations in doing it. Unless we affirm the possibility of translation, we give up any hope of communicating with one another. However, unless we see the limitations of our translations, we betray our language. Translation is a paradox that both affirms and denies the possibility of "carrying over" the meaning of words from one language into another. No translation can ever fully convey all the nuances, affections, and images associated with certain words, phrases, and sentences. Although we may find ways of approximating the meaning of certain words, they will never be exact. As a result, imagery and nuances are lost in our translations.[41] Similarly, translated words can acquire new and unintended meanings by virtue of other connotations implied in their new linguistic context.

Gustavo Pérez Firmat writes in his book *Life on the Hyphen* that in classical rhetoric, *traducio* was the term used for a word's being repeated with a changed meaning.[42] Translations always risk changing the original meaning of the work. Thus, the Italians have the expression: "*traduttore, traditore.*" It means that the translator betrays the text as well as the culture of the original language. It is interesting that the two words are so similar. The Latin *traducio* (translate) and *traditio* (handing over or betraying) share the prefix *trans* (carry over). However, while one word means "to lead or escort," the other means "to hand over." In the act of translation, we "escort" the meaning into its new context to safeguard it. In the act of betrayal, we hand it over. Both words imply that we are conveying something. But if we merely hand over a word to an alien context without ensuring that its meaning maintains the richness of its original context, we betray it. No wonder we often use the expression "a faithful translation" in speaking of a good translation! Translation is not merely finding a word in another language with an equivalent meaning. Rather, it is an art that, practiced well, conveys the richness and flavor that the words had in their original context. This art requires the translator to be intimately acquainted with both the original and the new linguistic and cultural contexts.

Pérez Firmat goes on to connect tradition and translation to highlight Cuban-Americans' shared cultural legacy (tradition) despite accommodation to the new cultural challenges of their location in the United States (translation).[43] Theologians also face a similar connection between translation and tradition in the task of doing theology. An element of translation is involved in handing down our theologies and traditions from one generation to another. As we pass on our faith, beliefs, and experiences to future generations, we "translate" tradition into another context. Sometimes these "translations" are literally from one language into another, but they are always from one context into another. The words and phrases that meant one thing for one generation may mean something different for another. Thus, theologies and doctrines are translated into new contexts.

Both betrayal and tradition have a common root in the Latin word *traditio*. Thus, in "handing over" we can be faithful to tradition, but we can also betray it.[44] It is interesting that both translation and tradition can be linked through the act of betrayal, for often we forget that our own theological traditions carry contexts and imageries that are lost when they are handed over to a new context or generation. As a result, we forget that our contemporary theological and liturgical traditions are also the products of an earlier context that may have been forgotten or overlooked today. Unless we ask how these traditions took shape in their original context and how they are changed in their new context, we also can fall prey to the tyranny of rigid and dogmatic traditions while ignoring their richness as a living heritage. Similarly, the words that emerge out of our theological traditions are also enmeshed in their original contexts. If we ignore those contexts as we translate our traditions into different languages, we too can betray our traditions by our translations.

By paying attention to the nuances and images that our culture and theological languages convey, we can enrich our understanding while recognizing our limitations. In a sense, we can recover the richness of meanings that may have been lost, as well as discover new possibilities for meaning. Similarly, we can prevent the tyranny of rigid interpretations that ignore the contexts and images that are unconsciously contained in the words we use to understand the living God.

The act of "translation" in this broader sense is also the task of the pastor in preaching, teaching, and counseling. In most of these activities, the pastors and teachers in our churches are "translating" the Bible and the doctrines of the church in a manner that makes them relevant to new circumstances. Unless we engage in this continual task of "translating" our theologies and our faith for the benefit of the church, doing theology risks becoming an irrelevant and futile exercise. Theology must interpret the Christian faith so that it is relevant to everyone. This does not mean that the academic pursuit of theology should lower its standards or that the academy should abandon its technical language. Rather, it means that academic theologians must be "bilingual" in another sense of the word, speaking both the language of the academy and the language of the people. And to be truly bilingual, one needs to go beyond translation. One must be able to think in both languages: academic and vernacular. Thus, theologians must be intimately aware of the social, historical, and cultural context of their time in addition to their academic setting.[45]

BEING BILINGUAL

In the act of translating we shift ideas from the framework of one language into the framework of another, but we can never shift the contexts that create the nuances and imagery that enliven words. As one American soft drink company discovered, these nuances can be disastrous. When the company translated its slogan, "Come alive with the drink of the next generation," into Chinese, the slogan rather unfortunately came out as "If you drink this, your ancestors will come back to life."

Certain English words such as *nice* and *chance* lack a direct equivalent in Spanish. The closest equivalents to *nice* in Spanish are words that mean "sympathetic," "pleasant," "good," and "agreeable," none of which means exactly the same as *nice*. The same is true with *chance*. The closest word we have is the equivalent of *opportunity*, which does not convey the element of luck inherent in the word *chance*. That is why many Spanish speakers acquainted with English use the English words *chance* and *nice* in the midst of a conversation in Spanish to get the proper "feel" or meaning. Thus, it is not unusual to hear someone say "*ella es muy nice*" (she is very nice). The equivalent words in Spanish do not have the same "feel."

Those who are intimately familiar with both languages find themselves continually shifting from one language to the other to attain the proper feel, imagery, and meaning. Often the result of this shifting back and forth is a mixture of expressions from both English and Spanish called "Spanglish." Thus, bilingual speakers familiar with both languages can convey shades of meaning missing in one language by resorting to the other. This allows them to become aware of connections, nuances, and differences in the two languages that might go unnoticed by others who are not bilingual.[46]

While not all Hispanics are fully bilingual, they are to some extent "bilingual" in their existence at the borderlands of different cultures that forces them not only to learn at least some words from the other culture but also to function in two different "worlds." Hispanics are "bilingual" not just in their ability to function in both languages but also in their ability to function in both cultures. This biculturalism, and even multiculturalism, is partial ly the result of almost a millennium of racial and cultural intermingling that has its origins in Spain itself. Hispanic theologians refer to this genetic, cultural, and religious mix prevalent in Hispanics as *mestizaje* or *mulatez*.[47]

The Spanish people themselves were already a mix of Moorish, Jewish, and European ancestry when they came to what is now the Americas. Through the inexpressible violence of the European conquest of the Americas, a new racial and cultural mixture occurred as the native inhabitants were forcibly blended into the Spanish world. As slaves were brought from Africa, additional mixtures of cultures, races, and religions took place. When the United States took the Southwest from Mexico, another mixture of cultures began, to which later were added Cubans, Puerto Ricans, and Central Americans. These mixtures created new multicultural identities that allow many Hispanics to bridge several cultures, functioning fully within all of them.[48]

Mestizaje and *mulatez* allow Hispanics to be "inside-outsiders" and "outside-insiders," having the separate perspectives of the two worlds they inhabit while combining them to form new realities.[49] This dual reality allows Hispanics to appreciate the similarities and differences of the various cultures they embody, and as a result they create bridges between these cultures and open new dimensions of reality that might otherwise be ignored by both. Being bilingual is one expression of this mixture of cultures that is part of Hispanic life. Our biculturalism and bilingualism allow us to appreciate the different perspectives, nuances, and imageries of these cultures. As a result, we are able to engage in a broader dialogue and enrich the perspectives of all the different cultures in which we participate.

The borderland existence of Hispanics also extends to the realm of religion. Hispanic religion often displays the influence of various religious traditions. This is not new to Christianity. Throughout its history, Christianity has borrowed symbols, traditions, and languages from different cultures and disciplines, adapting them to better articulate the faith. For instance, theologians at the dawn of the church used Greek philosophy to understand and explain their beliefs. They also borrowed rituals and imagery from Judaism and other religions to express their faith. Regardless of what we may think, Christianity is a *"mestizo-mulato"* religion.

The incorporation of new imageries and perspectives is a vital part of establishing a Christian identity—and being "bilingual" and "bicultural" is an asset in this process. An intimate familiarity with two cultures allows bilingual people to function fully in both without compromising the integrity of either. As a result, we need more "bilingual" theologians who can enrich our theological language and symbolism with imagery from different cultures while creating new theological perspectives. The "bilingual" theologian serves as a bridge between cultures, languages, and perspectives.

Furthermore, we need a form of "bilingualism" that can bridge the growing gap between the academy and the church. The connection to culture allows "bilingual" theologians to reach people at different levels and to communicate in different ways. As they work within the academic setting, Hispanic theologians often are simultaneously committed to the work of their church, with the result that they are able to relate to different aspects of religious faith beyond their own academic pursuits. In bridging academic language and the vernacular, they also can enrich both.

THE ENFLESHED WORD

Karl Barth rightly argues that our language about God should begin with language about Christ, for the Incarnation is God's revelation and union with humanity.[50] Christology provides us with the most accessible and concrete connection between humanity and divinity within the Christian faith. Christology is a *mestizaje* by which God and humanity come together to create a new reality. Christology connects God, language, culture, and human flesh in the incarnation of the divine *Logos*. Thus, the specific way we talk about Jesus should guide our more general language about God.

The way many Hispanics talk about Jesus is quite different from the way that most who speak English do. Our Spanish and Roman Catholic heritage affects us even if we no longer speak Spanish well or if we are no longer Catholic. Thus, in spite of our differences, many of us share a common Spanish Catholic heritage. For most of us, Jesus is immanently present in the world and an active concrete reality in our lives. Whether through sacred objects, rituals, and spaces, or through the indwelling presence of the Holy Spirit, most Hispanics understand Jesus as one who is near to us. In addition, our experiences, language, and faith make Jesus accessible to our everyday life. As in many other cultures and nationalities, Jesus is the one with whom we identify and through whom we have access to God.

In the person of Jesus we encounter the Christ and come face to face with the living God. Jesus is God for us, but he is also human. He is one who lives with us. He is one who understands our suffering and is close at hand when we are in need. We can identify with Jesus because he is one of us. In his death he understands our death and suffering. In his resurrection we encounter our hope that life will triumph in spite of the death and suffering that surround us. It is at the feet of Jesus that we must begin our theology.

In exploring the imagery, implications, and nuances conveyed by the Spanish language, we can enrich our understanding of

Christology and of God. Thus, we will see how Jesus is present in our life and culture today by examining how we experience him through our culture and our language. Beginning with the most immediate experiences and expressions of God's presence in our midst as love, we will move to the Incarnation, to the preexisting *Logos*, and finally we will return to the community of faith that embodies the hope for the kingdom of God.

As we will see in the chapters that follow, by examining these terms and experiences we can gain a new perspective and a vision of who God is for us all. Thus, in chapter 2 we can come to understand the significance of God's love as concretely expressed in our community of faith. In chapters 3 and 4, we come to understand Jesus as the "enmeated Verb," and finally in chapter 5 we can see how the community of faith embodies God. These tasks are what Hispanic theologians call us to do. They call us to begin by looking at the experiences and practices of our community of faith. They call us to look at the Bible from a fresh new perspective. They demand that we rethink theology. This book proposes to accomplish such a rethinking of theology by exploring Christology from a Hispanic perspective, both as experienced by the Hispanic community and as expressed through our language.

— 2 —

JESUS LOVES ME

"What did you say?" the elderly man asked with tears in his eyes. He sat hunched down in his wheelchair, his body withered by age and twisted by the ravages of a stroke. I was visiting a nursing home with a church group and had sat down to speak with him. "I want you to know that Jesus loves you and so do I," I repeated. He hugged me and sobbed, "Thank you, I didn't know if anyone cared anymore."

The troubling thing about my encounter with that elderly man was not just the abandonment and loneliness that he felt, but that like most people reared in a Christian church, I said those words almost automatically, without realizing the power inherent in them. Nor had I realized the power of God's love to become incarnate in my words and actions in spite of myself. That afternoon the mystery of God's love and incarnation became a little bit more real to me, and it made me wonder how God's love can still become incarnate, how the life of a Jewish carpenter who lived so long ago could still touch the lives of people today. It is with such questions that we begin our quest into Christology.

WHERE SHALL I BEGIN?

Ever since Jesus of Nazareth walked the dusty roads of Galilee, Samaria, and Judea two thousand years ago, we have had questions: Who was this man who lived so long ago in an occupied country, who taught about God's kingdom and God's love? Why was he tortured and killed upon a cross? What does his life and death have to do with us? As Christians, we believe that somehow God was uniquely present in this man's life, death, and resurrection. But how was God present and how does it affect us? These are some of the questions that Christology seeks to answer. For many Hispanics, the answers lie not just in the historical person who walked those dusty roads so long ago, but they are also in our everyday experiences and in our personal encounters with God. So we ask not only how God was present then but also how God is present now. The answers can be found in what God revealed in Jesus: God loves us enough to suffer with us, as one of us. This love that stands with us in solidarity comes to us incarnate in human flesh, words, and deeds.

In chapter 1, we established that Hispanic theologians often begin their theological reflection by examining human experience. Likewise, in choosing to examine the bicultural and bilingual experience of Hispanics, this Christology will begin with human experience and ascend toward understanding Jesus' divinity. But is human experience a proper place to begin our Christology?

It is, if we take both the Incarnation and Jesus' humanity seriously. If we do not, we are left with a Docetic Christ, a mere apparition devoid of any true humanity. That God comes to us in human form tells us something about God's revelation. It tells us that God's revelation does not occur *apart* from human experience. Rather, it occurs as *a part* of it.[1]

Our experiences are conditioned by our humanity. Our senses, language, rational capacity, and culture all condition what we experience. Ultimately, it is within this context of human experience and history—the only context available to us—that we encounter God.[2] And it is through it and within it that we attempt to grasp the significance of our encounter with God. As a result, both our encounter with God and our understanding of it inescapably occur within the human context. Anything beyond the realm of human experience is inaccessible to us. Thus, it is necessary for God to come to us in human form. Only in this way, a way adapted to our creaturely abilities, are we able to relate to God. It would be impossible for us to grasp the fullness of God's presence unless that presence were conditioned by humanity.[3] Most theologians agree that divine revelation needs to be mediated to us through a human agent.[4] However, they do not mean that all human experiences and all aspects of humanity necessarily reveal

God to us. Surely, they say, God is not revealed through a sadist, a ruthless dictator, or a murderer. Thus, while many theologians affirm the need for divine revelation to be mediated to us through human form, they limit this revelation to a particular human being: Jesus Christ.[5] According to them, humanity as a whole does not necessarily reveal God, only that One whom God has chosen does. Otherwise, they conclude, the result would be a God fashioned in our own image, created as the projection of our ideals and possibilities, and subject to the caprices and vicissitudes of human nature.[6] Therefore, they claim, only Jesus Christ perfectly reveals both God and humanity. Hence, Christ defines our humanity, not the other way around.[7]

They are right to some extent. Not *all* aspects of human experience reveal God. But neither should we conclude that *no* aspects of human experience reveal God. We should first establish a set of criteria for determining how and where we encounter God. Fortunately for us, we already have a basis for establishing these criteria in Jesus Christ. Christology inevitably pertains to Christ. As Christians, we believe that in the life, death, and resurrection of Jesus we encounter God. *What* this encounter reveals to us about God remains to be examined, as does also *where* and *how* we encounter Jesus. Yet *that* we encounter God through Jesus must be presupposed, or else there would be no point in writing about Christology.

Using Jesus Christ as a criterion for discerning how human experience reveals God means that human experiences should be examined in light of the standards set by the life, deeds, and message of Jesus Christ.[8] Establishing this set of criteria for judging human experience presents us with a further problem. As scholarly research into the life of Jesus has illustrated during this past century, it is very difficult to know details regarding the historical Jesus outside of the biblical message. Usually, the scholars who attempt to piece together a picture of the "true" historical Jesus—stripped of the accretions of faith—merely end up with a portrait of themselves.

All we have is an account of the life and message of Christ as perceived by his contemporaries and conveyed through the Scriptures. Ultimately, these accounts should be sufficient for us, for they attest to the impact Jesus' life had on those near him. These accounts also provide some insights into what aspects of

Jesus' life were perceived as divine revelation by his contemporaries.[9] Although the biblical accounts do not always coincide with each other, there are some things that we can affirm about Jesus.

Both Scripture and contemporary scholarship tend to indicate that Jesus preached a message of faith, love, and compassion that he also exemplified in his actions.[10] And both Scripture and scholars tend to indicate that Jesus advocated some level of social change that countered the established norms of society—such as the inclusion and empowerment of social outcasts.[11] Both also agree that Jesus' message ultimately led to his torture and execution at the hands of the authorities. Finally, as Scripture indicates, his disciples believed Jesus' life and presence did not cease with his death. Thus, we can conclude that Jesus' life exemplifies elements that are important to most people and to Hispanic life: faith, love, compassion, suffering, hope, and a desire for social change. By allowing us to compare our experiences with them, the characteristics we encounter in Jesus can serve as our guide for determining where and how God is present in humanity.

Using this criterion of conformity to Jesus' life allows for the possibility that God's presence in humanity may not be limited to Jesus Christ. After all, according to Scripture, humanity was originally created in the likeness and image of God (Gen. 1:26-27). Consequently, it should not surprise us that we can encounter God's presence in humanity. Although Adam, through his sin, marred this image, God's image is still an aspect of humanity, at least as a possibility. Jesus Christ, whom the apostle Paul compares to a second Adam, fully reveals to us this image of God originally inherent in humanity (Rom. 5:12-21; 1 Cor. 15:44-49; Col. 1:15, 3:10). Furthermore, through Jesus, Christians now are called to live in accordance with this "new" humanity as part of our salvation (Eph. 4:24), implying that this same possibility for mediating God is now inherent in us, too. If this possibility for encountering God is inherent in all of us, then it should be possible to encounter God through human experiences beyond those of Jesus of Nazareth. Thus, we do not need to deny our human ability to reveal God or God's ability to become incarnate in our words and deeds.

God's presence and God's love can still be mediated through humanity in particular circumstances patterned after the example of Jesus' life and death.[12] Thus, to claim that Jesus' life defines humanity does not negate our ability to encounter God in the midst of human experience. Humanity, as a whole, cannot be displaced as a site for God's revelation. On the contrary, the Incarnation affirms the possibility for us to encounter God's presence through humanity.[13] As we act in accordance with Jesus' life and message, we too can reveal God's presence in humanity, through our faithfulness.[14]

Nevertheless, most Christologies try to establish Jesus' uniqueness by setting him apart from the rest of humanity, by beginning with Jesus' divinity, and thus emphasizing the discontinuity between God and humanity.[15] In my mind, this is not the best approach to doing Christology. If we emphasize the discontinuity between Jesus' humanity and ours, we risk losing the full meaning of the Incarnation that the Council of Chalcedon sought to affirm by declaring that Jesus was of the same substance as God, fully human and fully divine. We also risk negating the human potential for following Jesus' example by setting Jesus completely apart from humanity as a whole.

Such a radical affirmation of the discontinuity between the human and the divine denies the full meaning of the Council of Chalcedon, potentially falling prey to Apollinarian heresies that deny that Jesus had a human soul and Docetic heresies that deny that Jesus even had human flesh! In addition, it preserves Jesus' uniqueness only by placing him and his ministry beyond human grasp. Obviously, this result would contradict the scriptures that command us to follow the example of Christ. If we are to follow Jesus' example, then there must be something accessible to humanity in the life of Jesus beyond a passive faith in its salvific value.

Traditionally, when Christology has treated the question of the person of Jesus—how divinity and humanity are present in him—it has assumed a radical dichotomy and discontinuity between the divine and human natures of Jesus. This assumption arises from our preconceived notions of divinity and humanity. As a result, even Chalcedon depicts humanity and divinity in terms of static essences that do not reflect our experiences of human growth or divine activity.[16] Rather than allowing Jesus to define for us both divinity and humanity, we have struggled to explain how our preconceived notions of both can coexist. Yet this need not be the case.

We do not need to accept notions that contrast the Greek metaphysical presuppositions of what it means to be divine with those of what it means to be human.[17] These notions drive a wedge between divinity and humanity, portraying God as an absolute, transcendent, exalted Spiritual Being beyond all suffering and mundane existence in contrast to all that is perceived as being human. The Incarnation ultimately forces us to reject this radical separation between divinity and humanity.[18] Rather than emphasizing the discontinuity between Jesus and humanity, we need to recognize that Jesus' uniqueness lies in the extent and fullness of God's presence in him.[19]

Instead of radically affirming Jesus' divinity at the expense of his humanity, Christology should begin with characteristics that both God and humans share, characteristics such as love or compassion.[20] In our capacity to love, both divinity and humanity find common ground. As the Latin American theologian Jon Sobrino maintains, it is essential that we show the continuity between Jesus and the rest of humanity, for in Jesus we find not only divinity but also true humanity.[21]

Love provides a nexus of humanity and divinity. By being common to both, love emphasizes the continuity between the human and the divine, opening the way for our Christology by providing us also with insights into God. According to Augustine, love is in itself a vestige of the Trinity, a remnant of God's image in humanity that provides us with insights for understanding God.[22] Citing the First Epistle of John 4:7, where we are told that God is love, Augustine argues that the Holy Spirit is the bond of love that exists between the Father and the Son. As we love one another, our love exemplifies the relationship between the Father (lover) and the Son (beloved), who are united by the Holy Spirit (love).[23] Augustine's understanding paves the way for using our own experiences and love as a window into understanding God. In the same way, we can use the Hispanic experience of love as an entrance into our understanding of God's love made manifest in Christ.

The Standard of Love

Christology is ultimately about God's love for humanity. As the twelfth-century theologian Peter Abelard argued, in the incarnation, life, death, and resurrection of Jesus, we see God's love concretely exemplified, in solidarity with humanity, empowering us to live in accordance with God's love.[24] As human beings, one of our most immediate experiences of God is love. In every respect, we understand God's relationship to us as being ultimately a relationship based upon love.[25] If this were not the case, why would God bother to intervene in human affairs to make them better?

We feel God's love for us not just as we hear about it in Scripture, but as we see it exemplified in Jesus' life and in the lives of others who follow him. We even experience God's love in our lives through those who act as vehicles of God's love and grace. We see God's love reflected in their care for us, in their compassion, and in their words.[26] In receiving God's grace, we find that God accepts us as we are in all our diversity and failings, unlike all those who discriminate against us. Instead of a God who identifies with those who seek to dominate us, we find a God who identifies with those who suffer—who does not dominate but works tenderly to empower everyone.[27] As a result, love is central to our understanding both God and God's relationship to humanity.[28] Since love lies at the juncture of humanity and divinity, it makes sense to begin our Christology there.

Love is central to the Christian message, as Scripture shows. For instance, love is at the core of the Gospel of John's definition of God's relationship to the world (John 3:16). Love also defines the nature of Jesus' relationship to his disciples (John 15:9-12). Love is the defining characteristic of God's being in the Johannine Epistles (1 John 4:7) and the basis of Jesus' commandments in the Synoptic Gospels (Matt. 22:37-39; Mark 12:30-31; Luke 10:27). The Scriptures indicate that love was central to Jesus' message and life. Furthermore, the Scriptures also indicate that Jesus believed that God was compassionate, caring, and loving enough to intervene in human affairs.[29] Throughout Scripture, love defines God's relationship to humanity and determines how we should act toward our neighbors.[30]

Ultimately, the Scriptures themselves provide us with a valuable definition of love. Not only do we find the definition in those often-cited words in 1 Corinthians 13, but also in the Gospel accounts of Jesus' life. God's love is patient, just, sacrificial, hopeful, and enduring. As we shall see, it is a love that transforms and empowers us.

In *The Model of Love*, Vincent Brümmer provides a useful paradigm for understanding God's love in terms of gift-love (*agape*) and need-love *(eros)*.[31] Need-love, exemplified in the works of Plato and Augustine, is primarily motivated by a desire to attain what we lack: ultimate happiness.[32] This does not necessarily make *eros* selfish and self-centered. In Plato's view, our desire is for the ultimate good, which also includes the good of others. In Augustine's view, what we lack and desire is God.[33] Thus, our love can be motivated by our need—the need for God—without being selfish love.

Traditionally, Christians understand God's love as being the self-giving gift-love that the Greeks called *agape*.[34] Brümmer illustrates the difference between need-love and gift-love through the work of the Swedish Lutheran theologian Anders Nygren. Citing Nygren, Brümmer concludes that while need-love recognizes some value in the object of love, gift-love creates and bestows value upon that object.[35]

According to Hispanic theologian Justo González, Jesus' life exemplifies this self-giving love, as evidenced by the Gospel passages that speak of Jesus' continual giving of himself to others. Ultimately, González adds that the Crucifixion is an active giving of Jesus' life for others (John 10:17-18). At the Crucifixion itself, Jesus' life is still directed toward others, to the extent that even while on the cross he prays for the forgiveness of those who are guilty of his murder (Luke 23:34).[36] Thus, González defines the essence of God as a love manifested in being-for-others, a love that reveals the fullness of both Jesus' divinity and his humanity.[37] This allows González to overcome the opposition between human nature and divine nature that often plagues christological formulations of how divinity and humanity coexist in the person of Jesus. Both natures coincide in the act of love.

Love, defined as being-for-others, bridges the distinction by abrogating the differences in the natures. Divine nature is not a static substance, as the Greeks and early Christians believed. Rather, our experiences of God's love lead us to believe that God's nature is a dynamic and creative activity of being-for-others that continually gives not only of itself but also of life, freedom, and the capacity to love to others while never exhausting its own possibilities for love.[38] Humanity, then, is called to reflect God's image by actively being-for-others. In our acts of love, human beings bear the image of God.[39] Thus, both humanity and divinity come together in the act of love for the other.

THE LANGUAGE OF LOVE

Socrates once said that "a life unexamined is not worth living."[40] If an unexamined life is not worth living, then an unexamined language is not worth speaking nor is an unexamined faith worth believing. Just as it did with the name of Jesus, the Spanish language provides me with a unique way of understanding God's love that is different from what I experience in English. Being bilingual, I am more acutely aware of these differences than a person who speaks only English or only Spanish. Thus, we shall examine them both.

According to Robert Brown in *Analyzing Love,* in English and in French no clear distinction exists between loving something and cherishing it.[41] In both of these languages *love* is a word that applies to most everything we like. We love our spouses and families. We also love our cars, our houses, our work, and our food. And in this list of persons and things that we love, we also find God.

Conceptually we might know that there is an acute difference between the love we have for a family member and our love of pizza. However, in practice, the word we use is the same. As a result, the word *love* loses some of its intimacy and significance. Slowly, our continual use of the same word erodes the conceptual distinction between loving someone and liking something.[42] Thus, it becomes rather easy for someone to say "I love you." After all, I also tell them that I love pizza, a good night's rest, and hiking in the mountains! It seems that love comes easily, at least as far as language is concerned.

The same is not true in Spanish. I find it very difficult to say *"te amo"* (I love you) to anyone other than my wife and God. In Spanish, the words *te amo* have a deeply intimate meaning. They are words reserved for a spouse or lover. To our parents, siblings, and friends we say *"te quiero,"* which literally means "I want you" but carries connotations of one's being dear and wanted. For things, we use the words *me gusta,* which have to do with taste and mean something akin to "I like," or more precisely, "it is to my liking."

Nevertheless, when it comes to God, we use those very intimate words: *te amo.* We use them to refer to God's love for us and we use them to speak about our love of God. It feels as natural to me to say them to God in prayer as to say them to my wife. Furthermore, there is also an interesting exception to the proscription against using *te amo* when speaking to others. Within the context of our faith, we can say *te amo* (I love you) to others. As with the elderly man in the nursing home, we can tell others that we love them in God's love. As a result, there is a sense of depth and intimacy when I speak of God's love in Spanish that I find absent in English. In Spanish, God's love seems more concrete and more real. In Spanish, there is a different feel to God's love.

Before my encounter with the elderly man at the nursing home, my nonchalant use of "religious" language had bred complacency in me. I told people that God loves them just as easily as I told them that I love pizza. My words became automatic responses said in haste and without thought. Slowly they eroded the significance of my faith, rendering it sterile and void of substance.

Yet, at the nursing home, I was surprised by the ability of God's love to be sufficiently present in my words to reach the elderly man in the wheelchair. I was surprised because God was able to do this in spite of me. I still had much to learn about God's love.

THE SOLIDARITY OF LOVE

Although expressions can become as trite and overused in Spanish as in any other language, there is an inherent sense of intimacy with God in the very structure of our language. For example, this sense of intimacy with God is reflected in the way we choose and use our words. For instance, Spanish, like Old English, still uses pronouns that convey respect. While in school, I would often get in trouble with my Cuban professor of Spanish for using the familiar *tú* (Thou) instead of the more proper *Usted* (You). As he would remind me during those slips, we could only use the familiar pronouns with our close relatives, our siblings, and our friends, and in some cases, not even with them. Yet, when it came to God, all of us, including this very same professor, would use the familiar pronoun!

It is also interesting to know that the English equivalent of the informal Spanish *tú* is actually *Thou* and not *you*. In Old English, *Thou*, akin to the German *du*, was the informal pronoun for the second person singular, while *you*, like the German *Sie*, was the formal.[43] What has happened is that *Thou*, being absolute and therefore reserved for God, practically reversed its meaning and became formal.[44] While in Spanish it is perfectly acceptable to use the familiar for God, in English the formality and respect accorded to God have led to the opposite practice. Instead of addressing God with the informal familiar pronoun, this English pronoun, by being used for God, became a formal pronoun!

In Spanish, there is a stronger sense of familiarity with God. Thus, our speech about God's love feels different. To say that there is a different "feel" to God's love in Spanish than in English may sound theologically imprecise from a traditional academic perspective. Yet it is probably the most precise manner in which we can speak about our experience and our language. When I speak of feeling in this sense, I do not mean merely an emotional experience. As the Hispanic theologian Roberto Goizueta argues, the Spanish word *sentir* (to feel) does not carry the intellect-affect dichotomy of the English word *feel*. Instead, it conveys an "experiential sort of knowledge, or perception, involving the whole person."[45] Latin American liberation theologian Gustavo Gutiérrez also writes of "feeling God differently."[46] What he means by this is that we "feel God" in the full context of the particular social, historical, and experiential situation in which people encounter and believe in God. Thus, to say that we feel God's love differently is to say that it is an embodied and empirical experience that acknowledges our particular experiences and the uniqueness of our cultural, social, and historical context. We feel an embodied sense of the immanence of God in the world and we speak to God in a more intimate way.

In a sense, Hispanics have experienced God's love differently. Like many others who are marginalized and oppressed, we understand God's love through our belief that God stands in solidarity with us. When we read the Scriptures, we see a parallel between the experiences of Jesus and our own experiences of marginalization, suffering, and death. Like many Hispanics who are born in geographical and cultural borderlands, Jesus was born in Galilee, a cultural and geographic borderland of his own time.[47] As a result of his Galilean birth, Jesus would have been belittled by the Romans, who held power in the region, because he was a Jew. But he also would have been marginalized by the Jewish establishment of Jerusalem for coming from a region that had not always adhered to the cultural and religious traditions of normative Judaism.[48] The

Judean people's feeling about Galileans is even evident in the Scriptures, when Nathanael, upon hearing about Jesus, wonders if anything good can come from that region (John 1:46).

Since Jesus came from a place at the margin of society and because he identified with those who were rejected and marginalized by society, we feel that God understands us.[49] But even more, through Jesus we understand God as one who accepts and identifies with those of us who have been rejected by the rest of society. Out of this sense of acceptance and solidarity, we feel empowered to claim Jesus as one of our own. This sense of solidarity deepens and intensifies our own sense of intimacy with God—a God who chose to enter conditions similar to our own.

The significance of this sense of solidarity and love for understanding Christology is certainly not new. Nor is it limited to the experience of Hispanics. Many Christians and theologians throughout the ages have been able to arrive at similar conclusions, seeing in the life and death of Jesus a parallel to their own life. As we have seen, God's love as exemplified through Jesus played a central role in the Christology of Peter Abelard. For him, Jesus reveals that God's love is in solidarity with humanity by uniting with human nature in life, suffering, and death.[50] But even Abelard's detractor, Bernard of Clairvaux, saw in Jesus' life and death a revelation of God's love.[51] For both of these theologians, it is by seeing this great display of God's love in Jesus Christ that we are moved and empowered by God to respond out of love and enter deeper into the folds of God's love.

However, for Hispanics the parallels between their experience and that of Jesus do not end with their reading of the Gospels. Instead, it is continually reenacted in their faith practices and popular religion. For example, in the *Pastorelas*, popular reenactments of the Scriptures that graphically depict the struggles between good and evil, only old, worn clothing can be used for the costumes. The old and discarded is chosen to symbolize God's choosing of that which has been rejected (Matt. 21:42; Mark 12:10; Luke 20:17).[52] In a concrete and dramatic fashion, this symbolizes God's acceptance and love for those rejected by society. Similarly, the reenactments of Jesus' Passion during Holy Week take on great significance for Catholic congregations and even some Protestant congregations, allowing them to identify deeply with Jesus' death and suffering. In a sense, as they reenact the Passion of Jesus, the participants feel that they are accompanying Jesus, just as Jesus accompanies them in their suffering.[53]

Through these re-creations that take place in popular religion, many Hispanics are continually reminded of God's love for the marginalized and the oppressed. Furthermore, they are empowered through these reenactments that affirm their belief in God's love standing in solidarity with them as they suffer. In a sense, the actors and participants themselves become embodiments of Jesus' love for the marginalized, the suffering, and the discarded. By identifying with Jesus, they also are affirming that Jesus identifies with them, and reminding us that in them we encounter God. In their acts of faith, they reveal and they preach the incarnate Christ.

But our understanding of God's love as present in solidarity with human suffering and marginalization is not limited to the power of reenactment. Within the Hispanic experience there is an even more direct connection between those who suffer and the presence of Jesus' love. As a teenager in Miami, while having lunch at my grandmother's house one day, I saw a homeless man walk by, pushing a shopping cart. The man, a Hispanic, was carrying various implements that he used for doing odd jobs in the neighborhood to earn money. As he walked by, I remember my grandmother saying to me, *"Mira al pobre cristiano"* (Look at that poor Christian).

As a young, fervent, and, at the time, misguided evangelical Baptist aspiring to be a pastor, I was surprised that my grandmother would assume that this man was a Christian. After all, he did not look as though he had made a confession of faith or darkened the inside of a church in years! It seemed that my grandmother was using the term "Christian" as an equivalent for "human being." As I went into my tirade of explaining why it was wrong to assume that everyone was a Christian, I missed the point of what she had said.

My grandmother used that expression only about those who were struggling, suffering, and outcast. It was not a word synonymous with humanity; rather, it was synonymous with *suffering* humanity.[54] My grandmother's expression was always modified by the adjective *pobre* (poor). The man who walked by the house that day was a Christian because he suffered. He was a Christian because he was in the likeness of Christ. He was a Christian because Jesus stood in solidarity with him in his suffering and alienation. I wish I had looked closer at that man, for maybe I would have seen Christ.

For Hispanics, Jesus is to be found in those places where people suffer and die.[55] The Gospels make clear to us where we can find Jesus. We find Jesus living in solidarity with the poor, the sick, the dying, the imprisoned, the marginalized, the hungry, and the oppressed (Matt. 25:31-46). Because Jesus identifies with those who suffer and who are marginalized, we know his love intimately. It is from this sense that Jesus is in solidarity with us and with others who suffer as we do that we can speak of God in so intimate a manner and feel such a sense of affinity with Jesus. And as we will see in chapter 3, this is one of the reasons why the Incarnation is so important to us as a symbol of God's immanence in human suffering.

INCARNATE LOVE

I remember listening to a popular rock song on my car stereo while I was in seminary. The lyrics in the chorus caught my attention: "I want to know what love is. I want you to show me." I was drawn to the lyrics for two reasons: First, most of us seem to ask that very same question at least once in our lives. We ask it because love is hard to define and even harder to understand. Second, the lyrics held at least a partial implied answer: Love is not just some vague, abstract feeling, but something that can be shown. It denotes a concrete act. Although we often speak of love as an abstract notion or as an uncontrollable emotion, we can identify love's presence only by pointing to particular instances and behaviors. Whenever we are asked how we know someone loves us, we inevitably resort to giving examples of things that they say and do. In a sense, love is always encountered not as an abstract, but in its concrete instantiation in particular acts.[56]

One of the greatest dangers we face when we speak or write about God's love is our tendency to render it tame by referring to it as an abstraction. Whenever we speak of God's love as an abstraction, it loses its power, becoming mere words devoid of actions or fruit.[57] However, God's love can never be an abstract ideal. God's love is always exemplified through concrete instantiations and actions that are quantifiable and demonstrable. As my encounter with the elderly man in the nursing home showed me, God's love is not an abstraction. Although my words themselves were empty when I said them, God's love was still able to reach the man through me, a flesh-and-blood human being.

In the Gospel accounts of Jesus' life, we see clear evidence that God's love for humanity always takes on a concrete and active dimension. Jesus' life is devoted to others in continual self-giving.[58] He is concerned about the needs of those around him and he takes action to meet their needs. When the crowds gather to hear him, he makes sure that they are fed (Mark 8:1-9) and feels compassion for them (Matt. 9:36). While others pass by the sick, the crippled, and the blind on the side of the road, he takes note of them (Matt. 9:35; John 9:1-7) and he heals them. Jesus' love takes concrete form and action. Jesus' life reveals a love for others that is active, concrete, and genuine.

However, Hispanics also encounter Jesus' love in a more immediate and incarnational form. We encounter Jesus' love as a reality that is mediated through the self-giving actions of others in our communities. The immediacy and immanence of Jesus in our lives is not simply encountered in the use of his name and in the concrete flesh-and-blood reality of those who bear his name as we saw in chapter 1. Jesus is also real in the love of the neighbors who come to our aid, even when it means that they must make sacrifices.[59] Jesus is real in the love and support that we receive from others in our community of faith.

To some, it may seem far-fetched to make a connection between Christology and the concrete reality of those acts of love and kindness. Yet we cannot separate Jesus of Nazareth, who lived and died so long ago, from the divine love and presence we encounter today in those who live according to his message of love, justice, and peace.[60] To deny the connection between them would be tantamount to denying the continual presence of the resurrected Christ in the church and in our midst.

The Empowerment of Love

This ability of God to become incarnate and manifest through our words and deeds in spite of ourselves is outstanding. That God's love is able to become incarnate in us and in our actions should not surprise us, even though it always surprises me. We are so fraught with our own sins, insecurities, and desires that it is already difficult enough to love others, much less ourselves. To act out of love instead of selfish desire appears to be beyond our ability. Indeed, it is so difficult that Augustine believed that it is impossible to do good or to act out of love without the empowerment of the Holy Spirit.[61]

It should not surprise us that Augustine understands the Holy Spirit as the source of love that empowers all our acts of charity. After all, he interprets the Spirit in terms of the bond of love between the Father and the Son.[62] And it is the Spirit, God present in us, who also empowers us to love one another.

For Hispanics, the idea that it is God who empowers us to love others is reflected in the words of a famous sonnet that states: *"No me mueve, mi Dios, para quererte"* (My God does not move me to love you). To interpret our acts of Christian love as being empowered by God allows us to recognize God as the true source of love and as the underlying reality behind all our acts of compassion. In this sense, we are concrete vehicles for the expression of God's love. God's love enables us to act with love toward others, often in spite of ourselves; and in these acts of compassion, these instances of selfless giving, it is God's love that empowers us to reach others. Thus, it is not a far reach for Hispanics to claim that God's love is immanently and concretely present in the acts of love and mercy of others.[63]

In our capacity to love one another, we see the image of God reflected in humanity, and thus we see the abiding presence of Jesus. As a result, God's love is not an abstract notion, but an incarnate reality. Just as it was an incarnate reality two thousand years ago in the life of a solitary carpenter in Palestine, it is also an incarnate reality today in those who mediate God's love concretely through their acts of love and mercy. For it is God who works through us to reach those in need of love and hope.

However, in speaking of God's love working through us to reach others, I do not mean that God's love somehow overpowers our will. Rather, God's love takes on our flesh-and-blood reality as it empowers us to do what we should, to love one another as God has loved us. The same love that acts in the midst of humanity through the life of Jesus of Nazareth also acts in us to empower our will to act with love toward others.[64]

Traditionally, divine providence is understood to work along-side human will in concurrence with our will *(concursus).*[65] God's love also works in similar fashion. It works through us and along-side us, not overpowering our will, but empowering our acts of love. As the many biblical commands that call us to love our neighbor, our enemies, and our God indicate, love is an act of the will. Love is not an uncontrollable emotion or an overpowering of the human will. Rather, it is something we can choose to enact or reject. Yet God's love can still manifest itself through us in spite of our conscious choices by revealing itself in our words or in our actions.

God's love empowers us to love others by providing us with an example of how we are to love. Thus, the incarnation, life, and crucifixion of Jesus serve to demonstrate to humanity the extent of God's love and empower us to follow Jesus' example in loving both God and others. So, our acts of love toward others are empowered by God's love for us. As a result, we are able to see in the love manifested through Jesus' humanity and in our sharing of God's love for others a revelation of God's love for us.

Yet God's love is not limited to empowering our acts of charity. Nor is God's love limited to Christians. We are still able to encounter God's love through flesh and blood. Just as Jesus' contemporaries encountered God through the life and actions of Jesus, we too can encounter God through the love and compassion of other human beings. As was evident in my encounter with the man in the nursing home, God's love can work in and through us to reach others in spite of ourselves.

According to the Swiss theologian Karl Barth, we can encounter God in the message of the Bible and in the preached word as it addresses us. I will go further and claim that we can also encounter God's love in the deeds and lives of other people, regardless of their faith and intentions. Yes, as Barth indicates and as my experiences demonstrate, Jesus can become incarnate in language and in our deeds, and so can his love. As we recognize God's love reaching out to us through the words, deeds, and love of others, we truly encounter God incarnate.

Finally, God's love also empowers us by bestowing value upon us.[66] Rather than loving us because of some inherent value that we possess, God's love for us makes us valuable, both in God's eyes and in others' eyes as well.[67] God's love is in itself creative, continually directed toward the other, on behalf of the other. Thus, our very existence is the fruit of God's love, creating us and bringing us to life.[68] Because our life and our being come from God, and because we are loved by God, we believe that God bestows value upon us. For Hispanics, knowing that God creates and bestows value upon us has several implications.

First, it means that all humanity shares in the value and dignity bestowed upon it by God. For Hispanics, this value given to us by God empowers us, giving us the knowledge that we are valued in God's eyes in spite of our marginalization by other human beings. In spite of the alienation and humiliation that many Hispanics feel at the hands of oppressors, we do matter. In spite of the ridicule and contempt with which others treat us, we do matter. We do matter because God loves us and bestows value and dignity upon us. The undocumented immigrant crossing the border at night in hope of a better life is just as important as the corporate magnates and so-called pillars of the community.[69] Thus, God's love that makes us valuable enables us to affirm our existence and value and empowers us to confront those who would deny us our dignity, value, and right to live.

The value God bestows upon us and God's demand that we love our neighbor as ourselves obligates us to oppose the forces that seek to deny these things to any part of humanity.[70] The notion that all of humanity has had bestowed upon it dignity and value from God also carries an ethical dimension.[71] For Hispanics, this ethical demand means that we must treat all people with love and respect, caring for their well-being and needs. It means that we must live in a way that affirms the existence and dignity of all creation as valued by God's love. Even if we do not always succeed at living in accordance with this moral demand that calls us to love others, we must try, for we know what it is like to suffer the indignities of oppression and prejudice. Sometimes we do forget to live up to these demands. Hispanics, like everyone else, are far from perfect. We do fail to live up to the standards of God's love. In many instances I have failed to love others as God demands. I failed in the nursing home. But we still must try. Not just Hispanics, but Christians as a whole must continue to oppose the dehumanizing and destructive powers of hatred and exploitation that rob us and all of creation of our dignity, value, and strength. As the noted Hispanic theologian Virgilio

Elizondo writes: "We must, as followers of Jesus, confront evil _wherever_ its dehumanizing and disfiguring power is at work."[72]

Since evil and its dehumanizing power know no bounds, all of us are called to confront its destructive power in ourselves, each other, and wherever else we may find it. We must acknowledge that no race or social status is immune to the destructive power of evil and hate. However, those of us who are marginalized and oppressed tend to suffer the brunt of this evil more directly and systematically than others, making us more aware of its destructive power. Because those in power often fail to see the destructive and dehumanizing effects of their own actions, we, who live in the margins, may be the only ones able to see and name this evil.

At the same time, we also are reminded that not everyone experiences God's love equally. Since God's love bestows value and dignity upon everyone, God's love also must take the side of those who are weak and powerless. Since those who have greater power can easily overpower the weak, impartiality would simply preserve the status quo of domination and oppression. A God who loves all must necessarily take the side of the weak and confront the strong to prevent them from destroying the weak. Even a mother who loves her children equally must take the side of the weakest child to prevent its harm at the hands of a stronger child.[73] In empowering us to confront evil and its dehumanizing powers, God's love must stand in solidarity with those who suffer from the forces that dominate, oppress, and often destroy those who are the weakest in our midst.

But not everyone experiences God's love equally. God's love comforts us, but it also confronts us when we become instruments of hate. This double nature of divine love is what South American liberation theologians mean when they speak about God's preferential option for the poor. They mean that God's love for all humanity requires that God call us to take the side of the weak and powerless and to oppose the structures that rob them of their dignity and life.[74]

Finally, as loved by God, human beings are able to return this love freely to God and to each other. The value bestowed upon us by God precludes any form of coercion. Love acts out of freedom and empowers our freedom to love.[75] This freedom also implies that God does not act upon humanity through coercion, but through persuasion.[76] In empowering us to love, God does not force us to love one another. Rather, God calls us to love others as we are loved by God. In loving us, God frees us to love.

God's love empowers us to love others by providing us with an example of how we are to love others. Thus, it is God's love demonstrated in Jesus that frees us to act out of love toward others. And it is this same divine love that becomes real to others through us. So our acts of love toward others are empowered by God's love for us. What Jesus reveals to us is God's infinite, self-giving love, incarnate in human form.[77] Through this empowerment, God not only bestows value upon us but also becomes real in the incarnate actions that reveal God's love for us.

However, through God's act of creation that bestows value and freedom upon humanity, God also becomes subject to the possibility of God's own rejection and suffering at the hands of God's beloved. The cross gives bitter testimony to the actualization of this possibility. In the life of Jesus, we are reminded that loving God and loving others requires taking on the risk of suffering and sacrifice. Although our sacrifices for the sake of love are never left in a void, they do exact a price. When out of God's love you share your food and money with those who hunger and lack, you risk going without. But you also reveal the incarnational power of God's love.

On the cross, God reveals the extent of God's love for humanity. Hispanics understand God's love for us primarily through our understanding of Jesus Christ. However, this is not an understanding of some abstract notion or disembodied presence. Rather, it is of a Jesus who is present concretely in our lives and in the lives of others. Thus, Jesus loves us because he comes to us as a caring neighbor. Jesus loves us because he understands our plight. Jesus loves us because he stands in solidarity with us, empowering us to love others and to be the incarnate reality of God's love made flesh.

Once, Karl Barth was asked to summarize his theology in a few words. After a little thought, the noted theologian responded: "Jesus loves me, this I know, for the Bible tells me so." This is also true for Hispanics. In the Gospels we see God's great love for humanity displayed in the life of Jesus. But we see it because in the life, suffering, and death of Jesus, we come to understand that God's love stands in solidarity with us. We see an affinity between the experiences of Jesus and those of many of our families, friends, and neighbors. But our experience of Jesus is not limited to those pages written so long ago. Jesus still comes to us in the flesh-and-blood reality of those who serve as instruments of God's love. As we shall see in the upcoming chapters, we encounter God's love through Jesus in an incarnate and active manner. Thus, for Hispanics, the question is not whether Jesus loves us, but how and where.

— 3 —

AND THE VERB BECAME FLESH

When I was a child, God was very real to me. I was born in Cuba under the communist government of Fidel Castro. Times were hard. Food, clothing, and medicines were often scarce. Electricity, water, and other utilities were in short supply. Although I did not realize it at the time, my parents often went without so that I would not go hungry. In spite of all I lacked, God was real to me in the love of my family and in the life of the church.

Across from our house stood the old town cathedral. I often played catch with the priests and watched from my balcony as the people went in to pray. As a child, my faith was simple, full of conviction and power. God was not an abstract concept or an intangible reality. God was real. I saw the whole world as sacred. God was real in the spring storms and in the night skies. God was a tangible reality at work in the world and in the people who came to that cathedral every day. In my eyes, God was really there with us.

One day I was surprised to see an unusually large crowd entering the cathedral. I had never seen so many people gather there, so I asked my mother why so many people were going to church on that particular day. My mother explained that they were going to church because it was Good Friday. I did not understand what that meant, and she explained that on Good Friday people remembered the day on which God's son was killed. I broke down and cried. Though I had heard the stories about Jesus and I cherished the thoughts of a living God who loved us enough to send his son to be with us, what my mother was telling me made no sense to me. I could not understand why anyone would want to kill God's son.

That night, people lined up in front of the cathedral. My parents and I went across the street to participate in the ceremony. Near the altar was a life-sized statue of the dead Jesus where the people lined up to kiss its feet. My parents took me by the hand and we joined the line to kiss the feet of this statue of the dead Jesus. As we got nearer, I finally was able to get a glimpse of this graphic image of a lifeless man, bloodied, bruised, and pierced. I knew it was a statue, but I could not bear to be near it. What had they done to my Jesus? What had they done to God? I began to cry.

Although my parents tried to persuade me, I refused to go and kiss the feet of a dead God. We slowly left the line as others kept going forward solemnly to kiss the bloodied and pierced feet of the dead Jesus. Since then, I have spent many years in universities and seminaries studying philosophy and theology. Yet it was there at the feet of this dead Jesus that my theology began. Although philosophy and critical reflection have enriched my theologizing, somehow I find that I must continually return to the experiences of those people whose faith led them to pray to a living God at the feet of a dead Jesus.[1]

THE INCARNATION IN HISPANIC LIFE AND CHRISTOLOGY

In chapter 2, I examined the importance of God's love for Hispanic Christology and concluded that for Hispanic Christians who experience God's love in a real way through the acts of others, the christological question is not whether God loves us, but where and how we experience that love. God's love is not merely an abstract notion but a concrete reality experienced through the loving acts of others. Through those concrete acts, God's love manifests itself. Thus, for us, God's love is ultimately incarnational.

The Incarnation is central not only to Hispanic Christology but to Christianity as a whole. Without the Incarnation it would be difficult for us to understand God's love for humanity in concrete and actual terms. It would also be difficult for most of us to believe that God truly understands and cares about human suffering. The concrete and incarnational locus of God's love makes the Incarnation an essential aspect of any Christology, and specifically of Hispanic Christology.

In spite of tendencies to spiritualize our doctrines and faith, Christianity cannot negate the physical reality of the Incarnation. The life of Jesus of Nazareth reveals God's ultimate concrete act of love and self-disclosure as occurring in human flesh. It reveals God's love for humanity through a human being and much more.

First, the Incarnation reveals to us the place where humanity encounters God—and it is a surprising place. Through countless ages, humanity has sought God in the heavens and high places. We expected to find God in the midst of awe-striking power and majesty, yet the Incarnation proved otherwise. God is not only in the distant heavens or in displays of power, God also appears fully as one of us. God does not come only in power and majesty but also in the humility of a stable. God encounters us through humanity, acting in its midst. Hispanics identify deeply with Jesus, not because of his divinity, but because of his humanity. In Jesus, God takes on a face of flesh and bone. Such a God we can understand; and we know that he can understand us, too.

Human beings can reflect the image of God in their loving actions, self-giving sacrifices, and concern for others. In all of us there is the possibility for bearing the image of God. In Jesus, God concretely brings about this possibility for becoming human.[2] If God can come to us in human form in this one instance, can it not also be possible in other instances as well? Although not incarnate in the same way, God can, nonetheless, become incarnate in us by working in and through us. As human beings, we can bear the image of God in our actions, languages, cultures, and history. As God works in and through us, we can freely bear God's image by our acquiescence and cooperation with God's work in us.[3]

Second, the Incarnation forces us to reconsider our values. Whereas society teaches us to value power and might, the Incarnation teaches us that the truly powerful need not display their power or hold others in their sway. When God comes, it is in the weakness of the flesh and the humility of a stable. Whereas many people value spirit and intellect above matter and flesh, the Incarnation teaches that fleshly human life is valuable to God. If human flesh is not alien to God's being, it should not be considered alien to us. God comes to humanity not as a transcendent Spirit or an immaterial presence, but as flesh and blood. In a sense, God is already present immanently in the created world, in our flesh and in our blood.[4]

God's immanent presence does not come as a surprise to Hispanics, since for us God is not just a transcendent, otherworldly spirit. Most Hispanics understand the world in a sacramental fashion in which God is often immanently and concretely present in creation. For some, this understanding is made evident in sacraments, holy places, and home altars. For others, it takes the form of the indwelling of the Holy Spirit, miracles, and prophetic utterances. For most, it takes the form of God's immanent presence in all the goodness of creation.

In the world around us we see concrete reminders of God's nurture, love, and power that mediate God's presence to us. Thus, for us, the material world is not devoid of God's spirit. Instead, while distinct from God, all of creation is permeated by God. Similarly, the statues of saints, the images of Jesus, the crucifix on the wall, the holy places are not just symbols—they are also much-needed concrete expressions and reminders of God's constant presence.[5] These sacred symbols mediate God's presence in a localized and special fashion that gives God's universal presence a concrete locus. In them, the abstract universals become concrete particulars, mediating God in a definite context in time and space.

Even for Hispanic Protestants, it is difficult to escape the sacramental nature of holy things. The Bible, the Eucharist, even the pastor all bear a semblance of sacredness in ways most find difficult to admit. The Incarnation reminds us that God speaks through concrete realities within time and space, binding together the spiritual and the material.[6] It reminds us that God's self-disclosure always comes to us embodied and mediated through concrete vessels.[7]

Within the Hispanic culture, we are constantly reminded of the importance of our physical and concrete realities as the place where we find God's activity and presence. Often we must also remind the church as a whole of the significance of the Incarnation and the value of physical existence. Thus, Hispanic theologians in the United States, like their Latin American counterparts, insist on expanding the significance of the Incarnation by taking seriously the experience of God as incarnate in human life.[8] This requires an expanded notion of the Incarnation that includes all instances revealing God's presence in the world, human experience, and history.[9]

As a result, many Hispanics who have experienced suffering in their lives tend to identify other instances of suffering, abandonment, struggle, and marginalization as potential places where we might also encounter God's presence. Similarly, we often see those who act out of love for others and struggle on their behalf as God's taking flesh through their actions and their lives. Ultimately, these aspects of Hispanic life confront the church as a whole with the reality of the Incarnation—a reality that forces us to take account of, and responsibility for, life in the here and now.

CHRISTOLOGY AS THE STRUGGLE OF LIFE

Within Hispanic cultures, the images of Jesus' suffering are often quite graphic. They depict Jesus writhing in agony, bloodied and broken, constantly reminding us of Jesus' suffering.[10] But they also remind us that God truly loves and understands us. They remind us of the struggle of life against death and of the value of life. Quite often, the graphic nature of these images prompts shock and criticism from other cultures that do not seem to understand the fascination Hispanics have with the crucified body of Christ. Yet this fascination is part of the legacy imparted through the Spanish-Catholic roots of most Hispanics. If you enter a cathedral in Spain or Mexico, you will likely find similarly graphic images; yet outside of cultures with historic ties to Spanish domination, these graphic and gory portrayals of Christ's suffering are rare.[11]

Spain's cultural and artistic fascination with death and suffering is a product of its history. Until they were unified through the marriage alliance of Isabella and Ferdinand, the different kingdoms of the Iberian peninsula were often at war with each other. In addition, until 1492, the same year Columbus came to the New World, most of Spain had been dominated by Moors for almost seven centuries. While the Moors' presence allowed many cultures to flourish in the region, it also complicated matters. Spanish Christians resented Islamic rule, often venting their resentment through violence. Yet Islamic rule also brought a true mix of cultures, foods, and languages to Spain. In addition, Islam's tolerance of Christianity, Zoroastrianism, and Judaism also provided opportunities for broader religious exchange. Thus, under Moorish rule, Spain underwent a cultural *mestizaje*, or more appropriately, a cultural *mulatez* that produced, among other things, the graphic images of Christ's torment, agony, and suffering.[12]

These graphic images of suffering were a mixture of the two cultures, symbolizing the suffering of a country often divided by war and displaying the influence of Islamic fatalism. Both the Spanish and Islamic cultures were ultimately resigned to enduring a life of hardship and death in this world, while awaiting a better life in the next.[13] One, a divided, resentful, and conquered nation, had little choice. The other, a kingdom governed by Islamic values, believed that everything that befell them was the result of *kismet*, or God's absolute will. Rather than being affected by abstract theological language that seemed artificial and devoid of life, they were more moved by the aesthetic images of tragic figures.[14] As a result, Spanish art and Spanish iconography were replete with graphic depictions of suffering and tragedy.[15]

Spanish fatalism was not entirely marked by hopeless resignation. The *Reconquista* that expelled the Moors from Spain was a prolonged and bloody campaign for all involved. The images of a suffering Christ expressed the Spanish Christians' hope that God too suffered with them and would one day vindicate them as God had vindicated Christ. Thus, the graphic images that permeated Spanish culture also held in them a sense of hope and an affirmation of life.[16] By contemplating images of death, the worshipers became more appreciative of the value of life and expressed their hope that their life would transcend their death. Although at first glance their hope appears to be otherworldly and morbid, it is rooted in a deep-seated affinity for life--and not necessarily just for life in heaven.

As the Spanish philosopher and poet Miguel de Unamuno maintains, the people's hope in an afterlife is indicative of a raw desire for life, with all its passions and struggles. But it is not necessarily just a heavenly life they yearn for, but also life as they knew it embodied in flesh and bones. The people's contemplation of the harsh reality of death exemplified in Spanish art, iconography, bullfights, and literature fueled their appreciation for life, as well as their passion and desire for a better life, not just in heaven but also on earth.[17]

The ritual I witnessed at the cathedral as a child in Cuba is common within Hispanic Catholicism. It is called *El Santo Entierro* (The

Holy Burial). On Good Friday, after a procession that reenacts Jesus' passion and crucifixion, the image of the dead body of Jesus is placed at the center of the church, where the faithful come to mourn his death and kiss the bloodied image of the dead Christ.[18] Hispanic theologians believe that the people are drawn to the feet of the crucified Jesus not because of a sick fascination with death and suffering but because they can identify with the suffering and death experienced by Christ. At the feet of Jesus they feel the hope of faith in a God who understands suffering and abandonment. In such a God they can trust. But there is more.

Though as a child contemplating the *Santo Entierro* I could not understand why anyone would want to kiss the feet of a dead Jesus, now I find it easier to comprehend. The people who worship at the feet of the dead Jesus are not worshiping an impotent and vanquished God, but one who lives and knows their struggles and suffering.[19] For only a God who has tasted death and suffering can really understand the depth of human sorrow felt at the feet of a tortured and broken body. And only in the face of the harsh reality of death can humanity truly come to appreciate and value life.[20] Even in Hispanic Protestant churches that shun the graphic images of crucifixes, there is still a particular fascination with the suffering of Jesus that is seen in sermons portraying Jesus' death with words as graphic as any image could be.

Here we find a key distinction between the experiences of Hispanic Catholicism and Hispanic Protestantism. While Hispanic Catholicism places a greater emphasis on the crucified Christ, Hispanic Protestantism tends to emphasize the empty cross—the resurrected Christ. This does not mean that Hispanic Catholicism only knows despair or that Hispanic Protestantism ignores suffering. There *is* an element of hope in Hispanic Catholicism and there is a recognition of suffering in Hispanic Protestantism. One only needs to go to a Catholic mass on Resurrection Sunday or to a Good Friday service in a Protestant church to recognize that the elements are there in both. In a sense they counterbalance each other, reminders that there is hope in the midst of suffering, that the Resurrection can only come after the Crucifixion, and that suffering still exists in our midst.

The Incarnation takes on a deeper significance for these people who struggle with their own embodied pain and suffering. They understand that God, incarnate in Jesus, intimately understands their suffering. Anyone who has endured suffering, torture, and oppression finds a deep connection with the crucified Christ, who stands in solidarity with all the countless victims of oppression and suffering in all places, cultures, and times, offering them a sense of dignity and reminding everyone that God suffers with all who suffer in our world.[21] And in Jesus' suffering, they also see the promise of the resurrection and vindication for which they long.

However, caution is also necessary when locating Christ's presence in suffering and death. Too much concern with the dead Christ and a spiritual resurrection can easily lead to a sense of fatalism and passivity that postpones action and life from this world to the next. Focusing on tragedy can easily become a way to idealizing martyrdom, passivity, and resignation to powerlessness.[22] This tragic fatalism can resign us to suffering in this world while we long for deliverance in the next. But these are not the sorrow and hope we find at the feet of Jesus; they are the passivity of the sepulcher that worships a dead and powerless God who is at the mercy of others.[23]

Miguel de Unamuno recognizes that the graphic images of the crucifixes and the dead Christ are not the same as the Christ of the sepulcher. The one to whom anguished believers pay homage is not the dead, passive Christ, but the active, living Christ who hangs on the cross in agony.[24] Similarly, in the rituals of the Holy Burial, believers focus not on the dead Christ whose sacrifice they honor with kisses, but on the living agony of the Virgin Mary who is at Jesus' side.[25] Although they honor Jesus as one who understands the suffering of humanity and as one who dies struggling on their behalf, believers do not worship death's passivity.

Spanish culture takes death seriously because it appreciates the value of life. It is fascinated with humanity's struggle against death and suffering—a struggle in which God joins us. Thus, in these rituals Hispanics worship before a Christ and a Virgin who suffer and agonize as they struggle against the forces that cause suffering and death. We worship God because we know God understands the depth of human agony as we understand it. We recognize that in the face of suffering, in the struggle of life and death, God is present with us. Just as God is present sacramentally in the Eucharist, God is present in the lives of those who suffer and agonize.[26]

Agony is not just suffering. It is a struggle for life in the face of death.[27] And life itself is a struggle.[28] People struggle with their decisions and their doubts. They struggle against insurmountable odds to live, to smile, and to create a future from a past and a present that often limits them. But in this struggle and agony there is life, and alongside us in the struggle for life we find God.

Thus, what brings Hispanics to worship at the foot of graphic images of Jesus' suffering is not the goriness of death, but the struggle of the living God—a God who struggles with death to bring forth life. In contemplating these images, we Hispanics are reassured that God understands and stands with us in our struggles. The images help us to feel empowered in our own struggles and engender in us a sense of hope in the face of suffering and death. Knowing that God is truly with us—Emmanuel—in struggling against death, we cannot help but worship the God of life.

God's identification with those who suffer does not mean that God condones suffering. We must resist any tendency to glorify suffering and martyrdom.[29] For this tendency easily leads to a justification of the powerful's controlling the poor and oppressed.[30] Such an emphasis would only affirm Karl Marx's accusations that religion is an opiate for the masses that lulls them into complacency by encouraging submission to conditions of suffering with only the promise of a future reward. Instead of justifying passivity, God's incarnate presence unmasks violence against the weak and the poor for what it is: violence against God.

The incarnate presence of God forces us to contend with our humanity. Through the Incarnation we discover that God is not in a faraway promised land on the other side of life; rather, God lives in our midst in the flesh-and-blood reality of our neighbors and the aliens who live among us (Matt. 25:24-36). In their suffering, God suffers. Through Jesus' incarnation, God reveals to humanity the image of God we bear in ourselves, forcing us to see God in each other. The Incarnation locates God's presence in the messy reality of life, and more specifically, it locates it in the struggle for life—both in those who struggle for their life and in those who through their caring love also struggle with them. The Incarnation reveals God to us through human flesh and forces us all to contend with the reality that whatever we do to the least among us, we do to God.

When Karl Barth centered his theology on Christ, he understood the central role played by the Incarnation. He also interpreted the Incarnation as God's objective revelation for humanity. Thus, we can know God, not as an undefinable abstract concept, but in human terms. In the Incarnation, God and humanity meet. By taking human flesh, God takes the initiative of defining how we can and should know God. The Incarnation is God's objective revelation that points us to God's presence within human history.[31]

While Barth defined his christological understanding in the philosophical category of a subject-object duality and limited it to the specific instance of Jesus, I will venture to go further. In chapter 2, I expanded the notion of the Incarnation beyond God's revelation in Jesus of Nazareth. God's incarnational power cannot be limited to a single historical event. God also works within humanity in all ages through God's love for us, empowering us to do God's will and receive God's revelation. Thus, through the power of the Holy Spirit, God's love can become concretely incarnate through us, acting in us to reach others.[32]

But I want to expand the notion of the Incarnation yet further. While God is incarnate among us in God's loving presence that acts within us to reach others, God also is incarnate among us in another way. In those who suffer and struggle for life, God is present as an object of history, as one who experienced human sin and oppression. In those who act out of love for others, in those who struggle for life, we see God as a historical subject, acting on behalf of others and as the creator and giver of life. Through those who suffer at the hands of others, God becomes incarnate as the object and recipient of the very real consequences of our sin. Through those who struggle on behalf of life, who act out of love and compassion for others, God becomes incarnate as a subjective agent of history, working to transform human history into God's kingdom, where love and justice reign.

UNMASKING SIN ON THE CROSS

The cross unmasks the violence and injustice of human sin and the sinful structures our sin produces. The Crucifixion forces us to confront death, torture, and humiliation. It points to those who truly are responsible for the suffering inherent in the human condition. I am always puzzled as to why theologians ask why God is silent at the cross or why God abandons Jesus in his moment of need since we do not ask ourselves why *we* are silent. Who nailed Jesus to the cross? Are we not the ones guilty of abandoning all who suffer at the hands of humanity? In view of our silence and passivity, how can we even dare to ask why God is silent and passive? Ultimately, the cross points to us and demands action from us to oppose the conditions that lead to death and suffering in our world. The cross unmasks our own sin by revealing our passive acceptance of, and therefore collusion with, others' sins.

The cross also unmasks whatever justifications we offer for oppression, murder, and destruction. Jesus was not gratuitously crucified. He was not the victim of a senseless, accidental murder. He was the handpicked target of the intentional machinations of the religious and political powers of his day.[33] And he was killed for very good reasons. In the eyes of the religious and political leaders, Jesus deserved to die as a blasphemer and a political agitator. The charges against him are similar to the charges all of us use to justify oppression of "troublemakers."

The Conquistadors used "just causes" to enslave and conquer the natives of this continent: they were liberating the natives from demonic religions and instructing them in the ways of the Christian God. The United States saw itself as the bearer of God's manifest destiny when it stole the lands that the Spanish had stolen from the natives. We deport immigrants today because they are "illegal" by our definition. We rationalize our wealth and others' poverty by claiming that poverty is the result of laziness and sin on the part of the poor, when in reality it is our own sin and oppression that has brought forth these conditions.[34]

The salvific power of Christ's cross is not its ability to expiate our sin or atone for our transgressions. To see God as exacting such a price from humanity or from Jesus is to paint a sadistic picture of God's justice as one that can be satisfied only by inflicting pain and suffering. Such a vision sees God's justice in terms of vengeance rather than love. God's love is not passive in the face of hatred and oppression. God's love confronts them and opposes them. God's love condemns injustice and hatred by exposing them and eradicating them, not by perpetuating suffering. The salvific power of the cross resides in its power to reveal the depth of God's love for us—a love that is willing to endure humiliation, suffering, and death at our own hands—and the depth of our sin.

The Incarnation and Justice

Locating Christology in human life means taking into consideration the social and political circumstances with which God identifies. Generally we tend to look for God in the "heavens." Traditional Christology tends to begin with an assumption of Christ's preexistence that puts him amidst the heavenly structures of divine power.[35] Thus, the inclination has been to understand Jesus primarily in divine, not human, terms.[36] This tendency has shifted most of the focus of theological discussion to otherworldly matters that identify Christ solely with the triumph and glory of the Resurrection, or with the preexistent Son of the Trinity.

Emphasizing Jesus' preexistence and resurrection pushes both Christology and theology to speculate about "heavenly" matters while ignoring the earthly realities that defined Jesus' life and ministry. In the end we fall prey to what the reformer Martin Luther called a "theology of glory," which speculates on matters of God's power, majesty, and dominion while neglecting the "theology of the cross" that reveals God's true power in love, suffering, and humility.[37]

In contrast to this emphasis on the glory, majesty, and power of God, Latin American liberation theologians place their attention on the pastoral concerns of Jesus of Nazareth. As a result, Latin American Christologies begin by identifying the particular historical settings in which Latin American Christians believe God continues to be present.[38] Latin American Christologies include Christ's presence in the broader "body" of Christ where the suffering of Jesus continues to be embodied in the lives of the poor and the oppressed.[39] Hispanic American theologians have expanded this notion to include those who are marginalized and excluded by society.[40] Within these contexts, the Incarnation takes on a larger meaning that transcends the earthly existence of Jesus of Nazareth to include human existence and even the whole of creation.

Because of the Incarnation, Christology also must contend with the historical realities of the world, including the suffering and oppression of the poor. Thus, the Incarnation forces theology and Christology to recognize that we do not live in a glorified world.[41] Like Latin American theologians, Hispanic theologians also see Christ's suffering as continuing in the lives of the poor, the sick, the hungry, and the orphans of our world.[42] Thus, the Incarnation is not only significant for a proper Christology, it is essential. The Incarnation forces us to take our gaze out of the clouds and look at human existence as the locus of God's activity. Yet, in spite of everything, we still forget that Christianity must contend not only with the spiritual needs of humanity but also with its physical needs.

WHERE'S THE BODY?

Some years ago a popular television commercial depicted an older woman ordering a hamburger in a restaurant owned by the advertiser's competitors and asking: "Where's the beef?" The point was that after you got past all the bread and dressing on the burger, there was very little meat. Today we can ask a similar question in respect to Christology. Once we get past all the theological dressings, we often need to ask: Where's the body?

Keeping Christology enmeshed in the flesh-and-blood existence of human life is essential to the survival of the Christian faith. Yet the body has been a problem for Christianity since the onset. Christianity was born in a cultural and religious milieu influenced by Greek philosophy, which viewed change and matter with suspicion. Since the time of Plato, the unstable material world was believed to be inferior to the changeless higher spiritual worlds of ideal existence. Thus, within the classical Greek worldview, salvation could be fully attained only by escaping the material world. From the very beginning the church fought countless heresies that wanted to separate Jesus from the flesh. After all, without a body it would be easier to sell him as the Christ, since no self-respecting deity would deem it fit to become entangled with something so base as human flesh. A theology focused on otherworldly realities was also more appealing to the complex sociopolitical world of the early Christian church, in that such a theology did not require them to try to change the structures of their society.[43]

Escaping the world was much easier than attempting to change it—and less likely to get you killed! It also seemed more logical to believe in higher spiritual and intellectual realities than to accept the "messiness," the desires, and the limitations of living as flesh-and-blood creatures. Being part of the transitory and conditioned existence of life in the flesh seemed beneath the status of such a "dignified" creature as a human!

Thus, Docetic heresies, which denied the flesh-and-blood reality of Jesus' human body in favor of a spiritual reality, abounded in Christianity. Subscribers to these theories could not believe that Jesus could really come in the flesh. Instead, some, such as Marcion of Pontus, believed that Jesus was a ghost; while others believed that his body was a mere chimera and his death just an act. Some even believed that the true Christ accompanied the human Jesus but did not partake in the affront of suffering and death. This made sense to them. It made their faith neat and easy and seemed to be a "logical" necessity for understanding that most troublesome christological question: How could God become flesh?

Yet, the Scriptures are clear that in Jesus, God was fully present in human flesh (Matt. 1:23; John 1:14; Phil. 2:7; Heb. 5:7). The New Testament and the early Christian church agreed that the fullness of the Incarnation in humanity was essential to their faith. In spite of the heresies that stated otherwise, the theologies that persevered in the second and third centuries agreed on the importance of Christ's full humanity. Theologians, such as Athanasius, believed that the flesh is corrupt solely as a result of our sin. Thus only through the full presence of God as flesh and spirit could the image of God be restored in humanity.[44] Others, such as Gregory of Nyssa, believed that nothing is alien to God except for evil, and that neither nature nor humanity is evil in itself. Thus, it is not beyond God's dignity or ability to enter humanity fully in the flesh since both heaven and earth are part of God's good creation, both valuable in themselves.[45]

Docetism persists as a tempting heresy today. It is still far easier to believe in a faraway spiritual reality than it is to face the realities of human life. Even today the image of Jesus prevalent in Christologies and other Christian doctrines still raises the question: Where is the body? When Christologies begin with Christ's preexistence and end with his resurrection, they tend to leave the Incarnation lost in the middle. The result is a fancy theological sandwich that leaves us wondering where the "meat" is.

Docetic tendencies are dangerous not only to Hispanics but to Christianity as a whole by creating a hierarchical dualism between the human spirit and the flesh that demeans the messy realities of our fleshly existence. This dualistic hierarchy justifies the oppression and exploitation of those who perform "inferior" manual labor, thus becoming an easy tool for the subjugation and oppression of the poor.[46]

By focusing on an otherworldly existence, modern-day Docetism mutes the cries for life from the oppressed and dying by promising a better life beyond this one. By trivializing work, nourishment, shelter, and other necessities for sustaining life in this world, it trivializes the needs of those who lack these necessities. Therefore, modern-day Docetism takes away the impetus to alleviate these unmet needs by focusing solely on the next life. By becoming more concerned with a person's destiny after death than with that person's well-being in this life, modern Docetism literally prepares people for death by contributing to the conditions that rob us of life. In denying our bodily realities and needs, Docetism leads to inaction and passivity in the face of death and suffering and ultimately denies life.

The faith of a people who worship at the feet of the bloodied and broken body of Christ makes it difficult to deny that God came to us in the flesh. Such is the faith of most Hispanics; it should also be the faith of the whole Christian church.

ENCARNACIÓN AND CARNE

Cultural imagery affirms the significance of the Incarnation through its emphasis on agony as the struggle for life. Similarly, our languages also can affect the way we think of the Incarnation. Since I am bilingual, I am well aware that the word *incarnation* in English does not have the same impact on me as the Spanish word *encarnación*. To me, the word *incarnation* is an abstract theological concept, while the word *encarnación* conveys a far richer concrete reality.

In English, the term *incarnation* remains primarily an abstract literary or theological concept. In Spanish, *encarnación*, like its English counterpart, can mean the taking on of flesh or the personification of an ideal, spirit, or concept. But it can mean other things. It can mean the piercing of the flesh with a weapon, or the formation of flesh as a wound heals. It can even mean an ingrown (*encarnada*) nail! As a verb, *encarnar* carries the sense of becoming flesh or being embedded in the flesh. *Encarnar* can even mean the *mixing* and *incorporation* of one thing with another.[47] In examining the words *incarnation* and *encarnación*, we discover that they are compound words, composed of a prefix and a noun, both fraught with meaning.

Although both *incarnation* and *encarnación* come from the same Latin root, the closest cognates in English are words such as *carnal, carnage, carnival, carrion,* or *carnivore.*[48] Unfortunately, these words often carry negative connotations. However, in Spanish, unlike English, the words associated with the Incarnation are not necessarily negative. For instance, in Mexico the Spanish word *carnal* can mean "brother," "close friend," or "family," indicating that a person is of the same flesh.

The Spanish use of *carnal* lacks the negative connotations of the English usage and enriches the significance of the Incarnation as the incorporation of humanity into God's family. When Spanish speakers read Paul's reference to Jesus as the firstborn among many brothers (Rom. 8:29), it makes sense. So do the passages in the Gospels of Matthew and John where Jesus refers to his disciples as "brothers." The Incarnation joins God and humanity in the same flesh, affirming that in partaking of the life and flesh of Jesus, we are children of God (John 1:12).[49] Jesus is our *carnal*, our brother who shares the same flesh we do, and we are his family.

In Spanish, the word *encarnación* is closer to our everyday language than its English counterpart. *Encarnación* is related to *carne*, a common word for "meat" or "flesh." Because English lacks this connection, the term *incarnation* loses its place in the everyday concrete realities of the flesh. The connection goes back to the Latin word *caro* (flesh or meat) and its genitive form, *carnis*, from which both *encarnación* and *carne* derive. This connection makes the Incarnation in Spanish, as it probably was in Latin, more concrete and fleshly. Rather than casting negative overtones on fleshly and carnal existence, *encarnación* provides a vital, positive connection to life in the here and now. Similarly, the Latin word *incarno*, from which we get the term *incarnation*, literally means "to cause flesh to grow," and more symbolically "to embody"—a meaning retained in the Spanish *encarnación*.[50]

The connection of *encarnación* to flesh and meat provides a greater range of imagery than its English counterpart. It carries a stronger meaning, akin to English words that do not exist—words such as "enfleshment" or "inmeatedness." Those words, if they existed, would be closer to the connection to flesh, blood, and life that *encarnación* conveys to me. When I think of *encarnación*, I can imagine myself visiting a cathedral and seeing the graphic images of a suffering Jesus. I can imagine banners in Spanish proclaiming the words of John 1:14: *"el Verbo se hizo carne"* (the Verb became flesh). I can imagine myself subsequently walking out into the streets of the *barrio* and seeing another sign above a butcher shop *(carnicería)* advertising a sale on *carne* (meat), while the *carnicero* (butcher) stands outside with his white apron splattered with blood next to slabs of meat *(carne)* hanging in public view. It is hard to ignore the realities of life in such places. The meat that sustains us comes at a high price, not just in human labor, but in the life taken from animals to sustain our own. In such a world outside of the *carnicería*, the full meaning of the In*carn*ation is hard to ignore.

The physical realities of our embodied life are important for most Hispanics. Whether it is our culture's affinity for life or the nature of our language that is responsible for our appreciation of embodied life is difficult to say. I suspect it is the result of both. Nevertheless, the realities of the flesh, of *la carne*, are always present to us. Words alone do not satisfy us. We crave the physical contact of an embrace that makes others present to us in the flesh, and hardly ever shrug off such an encounter. We celebrate life, enjoy the food that nourishes our body, feel the ache of our bones as we work, and are conscious of our embodied reality. This is not to say that others do not crave or feel these things. It is only that they are important and celebrated aspects of Hispanic culture. Life, embodied in flesh and blood, is not alien to us.

In Spanish, one possible meaning of *encarnar* (to become incarnate) is to grow flesh. Thus, when we say that God became incarnate, it can also mean that God "grew flesh." Using this meaning, the Incarnation is not just the indwelling of a human body by God's spirit, but God actually becoming human flesh! When we read the words of John 1:14 in Spanish, we understand that God did not enter the flesh as an alien intruder. Instead, the same God through whom all things are made also made "himself" flesh *(se hizo carne)*.[51] Just as God created our world and gave us life, God also made a place for the divine to be present within human flesh.[52] Thus, the Incarnation affirms that all human beings can bear the image of God *(imago dei)*. But it also affirms that this image is not just spiritual but also embodied in human flesh.

Thus *encarnación*, for me, carries a stronger connection to the meat we eat, the flesh of our bodies, and the blood running through our veins than the English word *incarnation*. It connects God to life in this world in a graphically concrete manner that empowers us to value our fleshly bodies as a place where God is found. The Incarnation counters Docetic tendencies and denies any dualistic hierarchy that devalues our existence as beings of flesh and blood. Instead, *encarnación* affirms that human beings are both spiritual and material beings.[53]

THE EUCHARISTIC DIMENSIONS OF LIFE

Just as the Incarnation affirms the sacramental presence of God in humanity, it can also affirm God's presence in all of creation. A sacrament is a material symbol of God through which God comes into communion with us, a symbol of God's material presence in the world.[54] But it is also a visceral experience. When we partake of the Eucharist, we eat it. It nourishes not only our soul but also, to a lesser extent, our body. The very words Jesus used at its institution imbue the Eucharist with meaning that connects it to his own flesh and blood, and by extension, to our own flesh and blood.

The Eucharist is both a spiritual and a visceral experience that nourishes our spirit and our flesh. In it we encounter God present in the acts of eating, sharing, and feeding—all important aspects of both Jesus' ministry and Hispanic experience. In partaking of the Eucharist we are reminded of the incarnate reality of Jesus' body and of his ministry to our bodies, not just spiritually but physically as well.

The connection between the Incarnation and the flesh is made vivid as the connection of the Incarnation and *carne* (meat or flesh) becomes explicit. The Eucharist connects the incarnational presence of God to the nurturing and sustaining of life. Just as what we eat and drink sustains our lives, so also God sustains us. We say that Jesus is the bread of life, but in the bread that represents his body, his *carne*, we can also say that he is the "meat" of life. In the life-giving process of nourishment, God is present. Ultimately, God is present in all forms of life-sustaining activities. Thus our refusal to participate in life-giving activities is a refusal to participate in God's work and in God's Eucharistic communion.

Conversely, when we deny food and drink to those who hunger and thirst, we are in a sense accomplices in their murder. This complicity need not be limited to directly withholding nourishment. By being passive participants in a society that robs others of sustenance, we too participate in the sin of that society. Similarly, when a society exploits the labor of others, it takes their lives away from them. As people work, they use their energy, time, and resources to provide a service or product. By putting their physical labor, time, energy, and resources into their work, they in effect pour their lives into it. In return for their labor, they should receive an equal portion of things that sustain their lives, such as food, drink, shelter, clothing, and the like. When their energy, time, and resources are not fully compensated, they are robbed of life.[55]

When we partake of the Eucharist, we not only are partaking of the life Jesus poured out for us, we also are participating in the life poured out by those who labored to produce the bread and the wine. In taking the bread and the wine, we are reminded that we participate not only in the life of God incarnate but also in the lives of those who labor to sustain our lives. The Eucharist reminds us that just as Jesus gave his life to sustain and nourish ours, so countless others also continually give of their life's labor to sustain our lives.

Hispanics, who have gone hungry and who have labored to produce food so that others might gorge themselves, are part of this Eucharistic communion that sustains others through their labors. I can only imagine what some of the people involved in the grape boycott led by Caesar Chavez may have felt when they took the wine of the Eucharist—wine that could easily have been made from the very grapes they were boycotting, grapes harvested at their expense.

When we give our thanks to God for the bread and the wine and for Jesus' sacrifice, we must also give thanks for all those who take part in nourishing and sustaining our life through their labor. In this greater sense, the Eucharist builds communion with other human beings as well as with God. As we partake of the bread and wine, we are not only participants in the body of Christ but also in the physical bodies of all those who sustain us through their labor, love, and sacrifice. As a result of our communion in the body of Christ, we are called to struggle alongside those who sustain us. Furthermore, we also are called to participate in life-giving activities, sharing our life and work with others so that they too might live.

The Incarnation not only locates God's activity in the physical world of flesh and blood, it also forces us to pay closer attention to that world. Both the Eucharist and the Incarnation concretely remind us that we cannot separate the spiritual and the physical, placing one above the other. They both come together, just as God comes to us in Spirit and in body, always mediated through and embodied in the concrete realities of creation.

Even the waters of baptism remind us of the life-giving properties of water, without which none can survive. But more vividly, the blood of the Eucharist and the waters of baptism serve as a symbol of life and a reminder of the processes of birth.[56] Through the Incarnation and the sacraments God continually reminds us that God also comes to us in concrete forms mediated by physical realities.[57] Given so many reminders, it is astounding that we still deny the value of physical existence, both our own and others'.

Often, when church leaders speak about life, they qualify and spiritualize it. They qualify life with modifiers such as "eternal" or "everlasting." They emphasize the "spiritual" life and oppose it to the body. However, in the Eucharist we eat bread and drink wine that nourish not only our spirits but also our physical bodies. If we acknowledge the spiritual nature of the Eucharist while forgetting the physical, we lose the Eucharist's full significance.[58] The Eucharist points us toward the importance of our physical needs— needs such as the need for nourishment. Like the Incarnation, when God comes to us as both spirit and flesh, the Eucharist also mediates God to us through the bread that sustains us and the wine that refreshes us. We must not forget that the material reality of the Eucharist is just as important as the spiritual. The Eucharist reminds us that we are not merely spiritual beings who can ignore our physical needs.

THE POLITICS OF FOOD

Both the Incarnation and the Eucharist point us further toward the value of physical existence. They remind us that God comes to us in concrete physical forms, and they force us to look not only at humanity's spiritual needs but its physical needs as well. As beings created out of flesh and blood, we cannot ignore our physical needs. All members of the body of Christ must be fed and nourished spiritually, but they also must be fed and nourished physically. One can never overshadow the other.

Culture, economy, and language play a role in the way we think about food, sustenance, and the physical universe. Just as the significance of the Incarnation can be lost in language, the connections among food, life, and sacrifice can be lost through language and politics. As our urban society becomes further removed from the land, from the growing of livestock, and from nature as a whole, we are in danger of losing the ability to understand the significance of much of our biblical imagery. Thus we risk not only misunderstanding the Bible but also further alienating ourselves from physical reality and from life itself. Although biblical images play an important part in our religious life, they often carry little meaning to today's urban dwellers.

When the Bible speaks of animals being slaughtered for food and offerings, it is difficult for us to envision the gushing of blood, the cries of the animal, the carnage and smell of death that accompany the image. Our imagery has been sanitized and packaged into religious metaphors, just as our meat has been wrapped in cellophane. However, for the writers of the Scriptures, these images were vivid realities of their everyday lives.

In our society, the larger share of agricultural work is done by Hispanics, most of them coming from Mexico and Central America. Through their work, our society sustains itself. We can say that Hispanics work to feed us. But more appropriately, we also can say that our society feeds itself on them. Along with other underpaid laborers from all races, the labor of many Hispanics sustains the rest of society. When they are exploited, we rob them of their life by eating the bread and wine stolen from them. We gorge ourselves on their bodies by gorging ourselves on the fruits of their physical labor.

Unlike urban dwellers, the people who work the land have a

more intimate connection with it. To them, the physical reality of life is more vivid than for those of us who live in the city. When we, who live in cities, shop, we go to a sterile environment in an air-conditioned grocery store. Absent are the smells of food cooking and rich spices. The produce is cleaned. Food is packaged in containers and meat is sealed in plastic wrappers. Everything is dead, processed, and labeled.

Those who work the land see it differently. In the fields and in their countries of origin, there is a close tie to the land, to the animals, and to concrete aspects of life. Streets and grocery stores are full of the smells of food cooking, of the blood of the *carnicerías* (butcher stores), and of the animals awaiting slaughter just outside. As they work in the fields, they see how the seasons affect the land and they see the fruits of their labor. Food comes from the earth and from living, breathing things. We eat the products of plants and animals that are alive. And we kill to survive. The meat we eat comes from the slaughter of animals. Ultimately and inescapably, life sustains itself through the taking of life.[59] Culturally we cannot escape the visceral reality of living as flesh and blood.

Food is part of our "enfleshed" reality. It is also part of our structures of oppression in ways reflected even in the English language. For example, we eat beef, mutton, veal, and venison. We know that beef comes from a cow, mutton from sheep, veal from calves, and venison from deer. But not even in the crudest steak houses do we find "cow" listed as an item on the menu! Why is it that we feel comfortable eating beef, mutton, veal, and venison, but find it difficult to say we eat cow, sheep, calf, and deer?

I suspect the answer lies in the history of the English language.[60] Words such as *cow, sheep, calf,* and *deer* come from the Anglo-Saxon language. Generally, the Saxons were the ones who worked the farms, raised the animals, and did the manual work. They were well-acquainted with the living, breathing animals that they raised and slaughtered. On the other hand, the words chosen for the food being eaten came from Old French and Latin, the languages primarily spoken by the Norman invaders of the British isle. In this sense, the English language reflects the socioeconomic politics of food.

The Anglo-Saxons who did the work and raised the animals used the name of the living, breathing animal, while the Norman conquerors who ate the fruits of the Anglo-Saxons' labor referred to the prepared meats only by their own words, words that became associated only with what was being eaten. The laborers who produced the food used the term for the living animal, while the conquerors who ate the animals used a word that came to designate only the food being consumed. Language such as this reveals the socioeconomic disparity that often occurs between those who produce food and those who only consume it.

In the Spanish language it is more difficult to find such a dichotomy between the terms used to refer to the living animal and the terms used to refer to them as food. The Spanish language thus retains a deeper connection between life and the food that sustains it. Hispanics who work the fields and farms are able to maintain a closer connection than English speakers have with the land and with the physical realities of life.

INCARNATION AS THE ULTIMATE *MESTIZAJE* AND *MULATEZ*

In the fifth century, the Council of Chalcedon affirmed that Jesus was both fully human and fully divine. Thus the leading theologians of the church resolved the controversies that had plagued them from the beginning. The affirmation of Chalcedon recognizes that in the Incarnation, God and humanity come together without one's minimizing the other. In Jesus, both divinity and humanity are fully present. In coming together, neither is lost or diminished, nor are they compartmentalized, stratified, or kept separate. Both come together in the person of Jesus while retaining their uniqueness. This doctrine requires us to affirm a paradox: that Jesus was fully human and fully divine. Yet in affirming such a paradox we also destroy the opposition of humanity and divinity by constructing a new reality.

This paradox is not difficult for Hispanics to understand, given our culture and our language. Most Hispanics know what it is like to hold different cultures, languages, races, and genes in tension within their own existence. Whether we admit it or not, Hispanics are a *mulato* and *mestizo* people. Cultures and languages came together in Spain, enriching one another with their diversity as European, Arabic, and African cultures, mixed with Jewish,

Islamic, and Christian religions. They came together through the violence of conquest and the pain of the Inquisition. But they also came together in marriages and in compromises. To this mix were added the indigenous peoples of the Americas through the violence of the American conquests, and more Africans through the iniquity of slavery. Through the policies of "manifest destiny" of the United States, once more another dimension was added to the mix.

The Spanish language also enriches our understanding of the christological paradox. One of the possible meanings of the verb *encarnar* (to be or become incarnate) is "to mix or incorporate" one thing into another. In this sense, the Incarnation incorporates divinity and humanity into each other, creating a new reality. Just like *mestizaje* and *mulatez* combine in Hispanics different traits, cultures, and races without dissolving their differences into sameness, the Incarnation joins human and divine natures without dissolving the uniqueness of their differences. As a result, both humanity and divinity come together to create a new reality that includes both while preserving their differences.[61] The Incarnation incorporates humanity into the life of God fully and concretely in the flesh. In the Incarnation, God has a human face of flesh and blood. At the same time, God is also incorporated into humanity. The two no longer share separate realities. Instead, they share a new reality in which both have come together. In this sense, Jesus is the ultimate *mestizo* and the ultimate *mulato*!

The new reality created by the Incarnation makes sense to Hispanics. As we recognize the different races and cultures embodied in our *mestizaje* and our *mulatez*, the biases and inequities of racism are harder to maintain. At present, globalization is making it more difficult to maintain an isolated view of culture and race. Although the constructs that divide humanity into separate races have always been questionable economic vehicles for oppression, they are impossible to defend in a *mestizo-mulato* world. Despite those who advocate preserving racial purity, we are inevitably headed to a global *mestizaje* and *mulatez*.

In the same manner that our *mestizaje* and our *mulatez* can one day dissolve the barriers of race and culture, the Incarnation dissolves the barriers between humanity and divinity. The Incarnation dissolves the radical discontinuity between humanity and God by creating a new reality that includes both.

In light of the Incarnation, it is impossible to maintain the radical discontinuity between humanity and divinity proposed by so many theologians such as Calvin and Barth—even when those positions are bolstered by the gravity of human sin. Yet the Incarnation also makes it equally untenable to maintain that humanity can attain divinity on its own. It is only through God's own initiative and action that this new reality can take place. But it takes place in human flesh.

The Incarnation demands that we ground our Christologies at the place where we encounter God: in the midst of human life. This means that all aspects of human life need to be taken seriously. It also means that life in flesh and blood, our own incarnate reality, must be taken seriously as the place where we can encounter God. As a result, the Incarnation forces all of us to reconsider our views of our bodily existence. Furthermore, it affirms that our existence as flesh and blood is a part of God's good creation—a part that is not alien to God.

— 4 —

GOD IS A VERB

The affections, images, and memories attached to the Spanish language we spoke at church still influence and affect my theology today. I realized this one day while I was reading a familiar passage in the Gospel of John. I was preparing a lecture on Christology and had looked up John's prologue to make a notation. As I read those familiar words, something began to gnaw at the edge of my conscious thought. There was a different "feel" to the passage I was reading: "In the beginning was the Word, and the Word was with God, and the Word was God" (John 1:1). I was unable to grasp the difference I felt until I reread the same passage in Spanish: *"En el principio era el Verbo..."* (In the beginning was the Verb...). In Spanish, Jesus was not the "Word." Jesus was the "Verb." Jesus was not just God's Word; Jesus was God's living and active Verb.

In an article entitled "God Is a Verb," Mary Daly argues that there is no reason to understand God as a noun. On the contrary, she says, reducing God to a noun is an act that makes God static by "murdering" the more personal and dynamic Verb.[1] Mary Daly's argument is not difficult for me to accept because I already thought of Jesus as a verb. Ever since I was a child, long before her article was published, I had read the familiar words of John 1:1 in Spanish, where it says that in the beginning was the "Verb" *(Verbo)*. Similarly, in our churches I saw banners and signs proclaiming that Jesus is God's incarnate Verb. References to Jesus as God's incarnate Verb saturate our liturgical language and permeate our imagination. The prayers and liturgies of the *posadas* festivals in Mexico, many Bible translations, and many Spanish theological texts all use "Verb" instead of "Word" in reference to Jesus. Spanish speakers have been referring to Jesus as a "Verb" for centuries! And if Jesus is God's presence incarnate in human flesh, then it stands to reason that God indeed is not a noun, but a Verb.

PRAXIS AND THE NEED FOR CHANGE IN THEOLOGY

If God is indeed a Verb, our theology needs to reflect God's active nature. Seeing the needs of those suffering under oppressive poverty in Latin America, liberation theologians created such a theology—a theology guided by action and praxis.[2] While liberation theologians do engage in critical reflection, they also reflect critically on the transforming activity of faith in God.[3] Thus, liberation theologies involve more than a process of critical reflections that analyze and examine the content of the Christian faith. They also require that we examine the way we practice our faith. As a result, for liberation theologians orthodoxy (right belief) is coupled with orthopraxis (right action) so that the former is judged by the latter.[4]

Liberation theologians do not propose a new theology, but a new way of *doing* theology. Liberation theologians give primacy to active dimensions of the Christian faith, using active verbs in developing their methodology: seeing, hearing, and doing.[5] Liberation theologians have become painfully aware of the reality of suffering and powerlessness by using social, historical, pastoral, and theological lenses to examine the human condition. In light of the plight of the people, they have begun to look and to hear anew the message of the Scriptures. As a result, they are driven to action as they seek to empower the powerless and to transform society.[6]

It is this action of empowerment and struggle for survival that ultimately defines the content of our faith—and the church itself.[7] The demands for justice and social change presented by liberation theology require more than ideas and conceptual truths disclosed through revelation. They require faith in a God who acts. The need for change and transformation at a societal level requires more than a church that believes. It requires a church that lives out its faith. Like their Latin American counterparts, Hispanic theologians also seek empowerment and struggle against the forces of marginalization, hegemony, and subjugation. They cannot accept the status quo in their struggle for justice, freedom, and liberation.[8]

Similarly, most Christians believe that God is more than just a concept or someone who watches from a distance. We believe that God is active in our lives, but we often become entangled in a theological quagmire of static abstractions that sap the life out of our faith. Yet, this need not be the case. If we just look more closely at the different images that language can provide, we can find active images that are better suited for understanding God in active terms. Equating Jesus with the incarnate Word of God is not necessarily wrong, but it can evoke static and conceptual images that, if left unqualified, limit our thoughts about God. If these static images and concepts become normative, our faith in God suffers by being reduced to a set of beliefs often devoid of actions.

Although our beliefs are an essential part of our faith, they are not all that faith encompasses. Our faith is much more than a set of beliefs. Beliefs are a product of our intellect, things we hold to be true even when evidence in their favor might be limited.[9] While faith includes our beliefs, it also entails a commitment, a risk, a way of being, and a way of living. It guides our actions and our life. Faith is more than a cognitive belief. Faith requires action.

Unfortunately, many people place more weight on what a person professes to believe than on what a person does, erroneously assuming that the latter necessarily follows from the former. But this is not always the case. On the contrary, what people do is more indicative of their true beliefs. If I were truly to believe that stepping on a particular spot would kill me, I would not step there unless I wanted to die. One's actions reveal one's faith.[10]

In light of our need for active, vibrant images of God, Spanish Bibles and liturgies provide a certain advantage over other languages by translating references to Jesus as God's Verb. When one speaks of Jesus as a Verb, as in Spanish, it is difficult to reduce faith to just belief without action. Verbs encompass both content and action. Naturally, one might say that a verb is still a type of word. This is true. But it is a type of word that we generally associate with action even when that action is conceptual. If I were to ask you to think of a word, most likely you would think of a noun. You would also tend to think of a word in more static and conceptual terms than if I asked you to think of a verb. On the other hand, a verb would likely evoke active and dynamic images in our minds.

CHRISTOLOGY AND PRAXIS

Speaking about Jesus as God's incarnate Verb creates new ways of envisioning both Jesus and God as active in human history. Throughout the earlier chapters I addressed the revelatory power of Jesus' life, love, and actions. Based upon these chapters, certain conclusions can be made about Jesus. First, *what* Jesus reveals about God is love. The content of Jesus' revelation is the extent and nature of God's love for humanity and all of creation. Second, *where* Jesus reveals God is in humanity. The place where Jesus reveals God's presence is within human flesh and human history. It is there that we must look for God. Third, Jesus not only reveals where but also *when* God is present. The content of Jesus' revelation qualifies the places in which we encounter it. Thus, while God *can* be present in humanity, God *is* present in those who act justly and compassionately out of their love for others. Similarly, God is present uniquely with those who suffer oppression and injustice at the hands of others, accompanying them in their suffering and identifying with them to the extent that their suffering is also God's suffering.

Now I turn my attention to *how* God is revealed in Jesus: as the one who acts concretely in human history out of love. God's revelation is not just a set of concepts, but a way of living. It is not just information; it is also action. It is not just *what* is revealed that matters, but also *how* it is revealed. Jesus' actions and our understanding of his relationship to God have serious implications for our own lives. Furthermore, Jesus' life and actions indicate how we should understand God's relationship with humanity and how God is present in humanity. God's love is not merely a feeling or an emotion. God's love reveals itself through concrete action.

As Christians, we believe not only that God acted in the life of Jesus of Nazareth but also that God still acts in our lives as well. It is through these actions, exemplified concretely in the flesh through Jesus' love and through God's incarnate presence in him, that we ultimately encounter God's presence in history and in humanity—a presence that is not limited to the historical person of Jesus of Nazareth.

What occurred in Jesus continues to occur to some extent in all of us. In the Scriptures we are told that Jesus is the firstborn of many who are to come. We are also called to be like Jesus. God can act in our lives just as God acted in the life of Jesus of Nazareth, working through us to bring love and healing to our world. But all this demands action. The God that Jesus reveals to us is not a transcendent essence or an esoteric ideal nature, but the God who acts in human history. To understand the God who acts, it is necessary to understand God as verb, not as noun.

FROM *LOGOS* TO *VERBO*

Spanish Bibles commonly translate *logos* as *Verbo* (Verb) when it refers to Jesus. Obviously, this particular translation can help us evoke active and dynamic images of both Jesus and God. Yet several questions arise. How did this translation come about? Is it a valid translation of *logos* in the New Testament?

Although the translation itself is unique, some of the reasons offered for such a translation are not really extraordinary. Rather, they are simply pragmatic. For instance, the current edition of the Reina-Valera Bible (1995), one of the most popular among Hispanic Protestants, indicates in the footnotes that it uses *Verbo* to distinguish between the written word of God *(palabra)* and the Christ *(Verbo)*. However, in spite of the pragmatic reason offered in the footnotes of this edition, the story behind this particular translation of *logos* is far more complex, and the reasons more significant, than it might first appear.

The story begins in the New Testament and its association of *logos* with Jesus and it continues in the works of theologians and translators throughout the centuries. It is a story that merits attention, for it can help us understand better the reasons translators and theologians give for calling Jesus God's incarnate *logos*. Ignoring the history behind the use of *logos* in the New Testament as a synonym for Jesus prevents us from seeing the value and significance of its unique Spanish translation as Verb.

The New Testament uses *logos* primarily to refer to words in general, to the written Word of God (Scriptures), to God's spoken word (prophecy), to wisdom, and to reason. Outside of vague references in Paul's epistles, John's Gospel (1:1, 14), John's first epistle (1:1; 5:7), and the book of Revelation (19:13), there are no other passages that clearly connect Jesus to God's *logos*. Since John's Gospel was probably the first to make a clear and explicit connection between Jesus and the *logos*, I will focus primarily on it.

The author of John's Gospel uses *logos* explicitly to refer to Jesus, not just as God's revelation to humanity but also as God's wisdom and creative activity. By connecting Jesus with wisdom, the Gospel's author associates the Christ event with a rich body of Hebrew wisdom literature and traditions, further asserting and solidifying the connection between Jesus and God.

In the wisdom traditions, God's wisdom is often personified as a woman and described as active in creation. Wisdom—personified as the female *Hokma* in Hebrew and *Sophia* in Greek translations of the Hebrew Bible—also serves as an intermediary between God and humanity. She abides with God, comes from God, brings light and life to the world, and is unique—all descriptions that John's Gospel applies not to a female Wisdom figure, but to Jesus. In addition, the wisdom traditions also portray Wisdom as rejected by humanity, just as John depicts Jesus.[11] Furthermore, there is ample evidence in the verses following John's prologue that the author intends to make a connection between Jesus and the creative, salvific, and intercessory power of God's wisdom.[12] But if he wants to highlight this connection, why does the author use *logos* instead of *sophia*, the Greek word most commonly associated with the wisdom tradition?

There are several possible reasons. One salient possibility is that *sophia* is grammatically a feminine noun that is personified as a woman in the tradition. Making such a direct connection to a male Jesus might have seemed impossible or otherwise problematic to the Gospel's author. Instead, he connects the grammatically male gender of *logos*, with its similar meaning, to the biological sex of Jesus, thus linking a grammatically male noun *(logos)* with a biologically male person.[13] Hence, the use of *logos* instead of *sophia*. It is also possible that John's Gospel uses *logos* to connect Jesus to the creative word of God. In the first creation account of Genesis, God creates simply by speaking. The author of John might have used *logos* to connect Jesus with God's spoken word that creates and structures the universe. In turn, this would also have appealed to Greek intellectuals influenced by Stoics who used *logos* to refer to the immanent governing principle in the cosmos.

Yet another explanation for John's use of *logos* may be found in the works of Philo, a first-century Jewish philosopher and chronicler. Interestingly enough, Philo uses *logos* to describe what is characteristically the work of *Sophia*. Philo portrays the *logos* as distinct from God and as the agent of God's work in history, bestowing it with titles such as "Son, King, Priest, and Only-Begotten."[14] Although some of these similarities may be attributed to interpolations of Philo's text made later by Christians, they still provide further evidence of the connection between *logos* and the wisdom tradition, at least in early Christianity, if not in Judaism.

Regardless of the Gospel writer's intent in using *logos* instead of *sophia,* this usage establishes a connection between Jesus and the wisdom tradition—with its concrete personification of Wisdom and her creative activity. If this connection is indeed the case, then the creative and active dimensions of wisdom's personification as *Sophia* are applicable to Jesus as the *Logos.* Thus, it is possible to assert that Jesus' revelation consists of more than just cognitive information about God and our relationship to God. It also has an active dimension. The *Logos* reveals God's love in action by giving life through the redeeming work of Jesus and in the act of creation.[15] Based solely on this interpretation, an active understanding of God's revelation in Jesus is not only possible but desirable.

In John's Gospel, the connection between the person of Jesus and the revelation he brings are so intricate that the revelation cannot be reduced to just his words. The revelation also encompasses his coming and his actions.[16] If this is the case, then the Spanish translation of *logos* as *Verbo* (Verb) is a plausible translation that does not betray the text by alluding to the active and communicative nature of God's revelation. On the contrary, it preserves the active and dynamic nature of God's work in Jesus of Nazareth. However, the story does not end here. In the centuries that followed, other writers and theologians also interpreted *logos* as active and dynamic, lending further credence to translating it by using words that express not only cognition but also action.

Less than a century after John's Gospel was written, the association of the *logos* with God's creative word became more explicit in the works of some of the earliest Christian theologians. Justin Martyr, for instance, one of the first theologians to use a philosophical approach to theology, also equates Jesus of Nazareth with the *logos*. In his writings, as in John's Gospel, the *logos* preexisted along with God, serving as a mediator between God and humanity and participating in the creative act.[17] Whether Justin was actually indebted to Middle Platonism and Stoic philosophy in developing his *logos* Christology is questionable.[18] It is entirely possible that Justin was just as indebted to the Jewish wisdom tradition and to Philo's works, which would have been known to Justin and other Christians of the era. Regardless of his source, Justin stil portrays the *logos* both as law and as an active power.[19] Again, this indicates the plausibility of translating *logos* in active terms, allowing for the validity of the Spanish translation of it as Verb.

The story continues a few decades later. When Tertullian developed his model for understanding the Trinity as three persons sharing one divine substance, he also connected the *logos* with the act of creation. Writing in Latin, he translated *logos* into two different yet related words: *ratio* (reason) and *sermo* (spoken word). Although Tertullian could have easily used the Latin word *verbum*, which can mean either "word" or "verb," he does not. At first glance, this might seem to counter my argument in favor of translating *logos* as verb, but it does not. There are several reasons why Tertullian might have chosen his particular translation that do not take away from an active understanding of *logos*.

One possibility is that because the grammatical gender of *verbum* is neutral—neither masculine nor feminine—Tertullian preferred masculine terms to make an explicit connection to Jesus' gender.[20] It is even more likely that Tertullian used *sermo* and *ratio* to be able to make the distinction he sought between the spoken word and reason. Making this distinction made easier Tertullian's argument against the Monarchian heresy, a modalist heresy that rejected any trinitarian distinctions. This distinction allowed Tertullian to distinguish between reason, which was present in God as thought, and God's spoken word, which became distinct from God in the act of creation.[21] This allowed him to argue that Jesus' divinity could be related to God's own divinity while being distinct, an essential part of his trinitarian understanding.

In spite of his word choice, Tertullian still maintains an active understanding of *logos* in his translation. The spoken word, which he associates with Christ, is active in creation. God's spoken word is not merely a noun. It is dynamic and creative. The *logos* does more than describe and define reality. It constructs reality. Thus, translating it in active terms, as is done in Spanish, is true to the understanding of early theologians such as Tertullian.

Later in the Vulgate and other Latin translations of the Bible, *logos* becomes *verbum* when referring to Jesus. *Verbum*, like *logos*, also has multiple meanings. Like its Greek counterpart it too can mean both "word" or "verb." It is from *verbum* that we get such words in the English language as *verb*, *verbal*, and *verbose*. Thus, in the Latin translation the reference to Christ as *Verbum* can convey not just communication from God but also God's activity in Jesus.

Throughout the centuries that followed, the Latin church used the Vulgate as the normative translation. Even though the luxury of reading the Scriptures was reserved for scholars and clerics, the words of the Vulgate became entrenched in the liturgy of the church and in the minds of those who could still understand Latin.

It was not until decades after the Reformation that the first translations of the Bible into Spanish appeared. The earliest of these translations, by Casidoro de Reina (1569) and Cipriano Valera (1600), translated the Greek *logos* as *Palabra* (Word) in a fashion similar to the earlier English translations. Considering that they were in England during the time they accomplished most of their work, that both were Protestant, and that they were trying to faithfully translate from the original Greek, it is not surprising that they translated *logos* in that fashion. Yet, a Spanish New Testament that dates to 1556 translates *logos* as *palabra*, but has *verbo* written in ink in the margins! It was not until 1793, when Felipe Scio de San Miguel first translated the Latin Vulgate into Spanish with the consent of the Spanish king, that *Verbo* first appeared in Spanish as a translation for God's incarnate *logos*.

Felipe Scio de San Miguel made no qualms about his love of the Spanish language. He actually felt that Spanish was better suited to convey the intricacies and subtleties of meaning found in the original biblical language and in the officially accepted Latin text than any other language.[22] Furthermore, to avoid any problems with the Catholic Church, his translation followed closely the Latin text of the Vulgate, a text that uses *Verbum* to translate references to Jesus as *logos*. Thus, when Scio de San Miguel translated it into Spanish, he translated it as *Verbo* to remain more faithful to the Latin text. He also mentioned in his comments that he used *Verbo* to distinguish between passages that refer to the Second Person of the Trinity and passages that refer to the written word of God.[23]

In 1813 a version of the New Testament published in Spanish by Diego Powell also used *Verbo* to refer to Jesus; but unlike his predecessor, Powell gave no indication as to why he chose that particular translation. A little over two decades later, in 1835, Felix Torres Amat published his new translation of the Bible in the Americas. It was the first Spanish translation of the Bible published in the New World and quickly became the Bible of choice in the Americas among Spanish-speaking Catholics and Protestants alike.

In Amat's Bible we encounter an additional reason for choosing to use *Verb* in place of *Word*. Torres Amat is familiar with Scio de San Miguel's translation, as well as others. Like his predecessors, Amat is also familiar with both the Greek and the Latin versions. Yet he chooses to follow Scio de San Miguel's translation of *logos* as *Verbo*. Although Amat is also a Catholic seeking to preserve a link to the Vulgate, he does not choose this particular translation solely for the same reasons as Scio de San Miguel.

In his glossary, Amat explains that translating *logos* as *Verbo* is not only antonomastic but the only possible way to denote the act of God in Christ.[24] Thus for Torres Amat, the translation is not merely an attempt to parallel the flexibility of the Latin *Verbum* in order to make a distinction between the written Word of God and Christ. It is also a way of conveying God's activity in Christ. According to Torres Amat, he seeks to preserve in his translation the richness of the Greek word *logos* as used in the New Testament to refer to Jesus.

Amat's Bible became quite popular not just among Catholics but also among Spanish-speaking Protestants in the Americas. The popularity of this translation eventually led to a proliferation of references to Jesus as God's incarnate Verb in liturgy and popular parlance alike. Soon other translations began to use *Verbo* in John's Gospel, including later revisions of the Reina-Valera translation (1862, 1900, 1960, 1995). Similarly, the use of *Verbo* in reference to Christ grew more common in the rituals, signs, and banners of both Catholic and Protestant Spanish-speaking churches. This proliferation of references to Jesus as God's incarnate Verb in Spanish-speaking churches helps those of us who grew up with them to understand God in active terms. It also provides fertile ground for the development of Christologies and theologies that place a greater emphasis on action over theory. Ultimately, it can help Christianity rediscover the biblical God—the God who acts in history.

AN ACT OF GOD

Today when we hear the term "an act of God," we generally associate it with some form of natural calamity. We make this association because insurance companies, not churches, use it to describe the disastrous consequences of natural phenomena. Unfortunately, churches have allowed insurance companies to take over this term and preempt its ecclesial use. This does not mean that churches have proprietary rights to this particular term or that insurance agents have inappropriately usurped it from the churches. Rather, it means that insurance companies seem to use the term more frequently than churches, so that an "act of God" as defined in insurance parlance is more widely understood than an "act of God" as defined in the Bible.

The Bible clearly portrays God as an active agent of history, not as a passive observer. From the very beginning, God is present in history as its creator. In the first creation account of Genesis, God creates the heavens and the earth. Actually, in the original Hebrew text, the word order itself speaks of God's act before it even mentions God: "In the beginning created God..." (Gen. 1:1). The remaining passages portray God as moving over the waters, seeing, speaking, and creating. Similarly, the rest of the Hebrew Scriptures also portray God as judging and redeeming human history by acting and intervening in it. God is not a passive observer but an active participant who interacts with humanity and demands that we, too, act in a just and loving manner. This God who loves us and acts in history is the God Jesus reveals to us.

The New Testament takes God's activity to a new level by locating it within humanity itself. In the New Testament, what attests to Jesus' divinity are his actions.[25] He does not have a divine aura that surrounds him, nor do his words unambiguously indicate his divinity. After all, not everyone believed in him. Thus, the writers of the New Testament do not concern themselves so much with questions about the person of Jesus—that is, his divine nature or substance. Instead, they are concerned with Jesus' deeds, proclamations, miracles, and salvific actions.[26] In other words, what Jesus does takes precedence over who he is, and what he does in fact discloses his divinity. Through his deeds we come to believe that he is God.

The New Testament portrays Jesus not just as a teacher but also as a man of action—Jesus' deeds and miracles are as much a part of his proclamation as his words. His miracles are acts of power that not only proclaim God's kingdom on earth but also make it a reality.[27] When Jesus sees a need, he takes action. When he sees the multitudes that have gathered to hear him, he makes sure that they are fed (Matt. 14:16; Mark 6:37; Luke 9:13). He recognizes both the spiritual and the physical needs of the ill and heals them (Matt. 4:23; 9:35). Even his words are characterized by the way he speaks them. Thus, people are astonished not only by the content of his message but by the authority inherent in it (Matt. 7:29; Mark 1:22; Luke 4:32).

Jesus proclaimed the coming of the Kingdom, but he also sought to bring it about by changing human lives and the rules that govern them.[28] No one who studies Jesus' ministry can justify a proclamation of God's kingdom that is devoid of actions that make the Kingdom a reality. Nor can they justify deferring their actions and the realization of God's kingdom to a future age or time. Jesus' own actions and his emphasis on action in his preaching were important aspects of his life and work. Throughout his life, Jesus was constantly on the move and directed his disciples to take action. Jesus does not expect his disciples to stand in beatific contemplation of his glory, but to go out and minister to others.

Jesus' actions were compassionate toward those who suffered from affliction and injustice, but his actions were sharp against those who caused them. Although he recognized the danger involved in challenging unjust power structures, he still denounced them, putting his life at risk for the sake of others and facing death for the sake of his calling. While many might imagine Jesus as a meek and passive individual who exudes a radiant light, that is not how the New Testament pictures him. The Jesus we find in its stories takes a stand against unjust practices and takes a whip against the money changers in the Temple. The Jesus of the Gospels—the Jesus to whom we Hispanics cleave—is a Jesus who does not shy away from conflict, who demands justice for the oppressed, and who calls the church to confront the sinful structures of our world.[29] While conformity and the deferral of action often seem safer routes in the face of injustice and evil, the God who acts in history calls us to confront those who perpetrate evil in our society. Just as Jesus takes the risk of confronting the centers of power in Jerusalem, so also he calls his church to confront sinful structures that deprive humanity of dignity and life.[30]

Jesus' divine activity does not detract from his humanity. Although he performs miracles, his actions are often those that anyone moved by compassion would do. In facing death, he displays typical human emotions. He is vulnerable, weeping at Lazarus' tomb (John 11:30-38) and at the Garden of Gethsemane (Matt. 26:14-46; Mark 14:32-42; Luke 22:39-46; John 18:1). Yet he takes strength from his faith and his commitment to do whatever is necessary to give life to humanity and the whole world, including facing his own death.

Jesus' death does not curtail his activity in the world. The Gospels indicate that the resurrected Christ continues to act concretely in history. The Scriptures present the Resurrection as a transformation. The Resurrection transforms Jesus' death and vanquishment into life and victory. Death does not halt his concrete and active impact on the world. Jesus' work continues enfleshed in humanity in a new manner. The Resurrection reminds us that the locus of God's activity and presence continues to be in the midst of human history and human flesh even after Jesus' death.

The Resurrection confirms that the continuing activity of the resurrected Christ in history occurs through a bodily reality. The authors of the New Testament take great pains to indicate to us that the resurrected Christ is not an apparition or phantasm; but he is changed. Based upon his appearance alone, Jesus is not immediately recognized by those who knew him before the resurrection.[31] Rather, he is recognized by how he speaks and how he acts. But it is not the recognition of Jesus' physical and bodily traits that confirms his resurrection, nor is it his being or substance that the disciples recognize. What reveals Jesus as the risen Christ are his actions. Through the continuity of his concrete actions—past, present, and future—Jesus becomes manifest as the resurrected Christ.

In Luke's account, for instance, the travelers on the road to Emmaus do not recognize their companion as Jesus until he breaks the bread and shares it with them as he had done so many times before the Resurrection (Luke 24:13-35). The act of breaking the bread is what reminds them of the Lord's supper, with all its implications of sharing and nourishing both the physical and spiritual needs of our bodies. Although Jesus' words "burn" in their hearts as he speaks, it is the act of breaking the bread itself that reveals him as the resurrected Christ (Luke 24:35).[32] In the Eucharist, Jesus' resurrection is proclaimed. In sharing the elements that nourish both our body and spirit, Jesus' resurrected presence becomes a reality. The resurrected Christ still continues to act through us in our rituals, in our sharing, in our feeding of the masses, and in our provision for the needs of those who lack.

Later, when Jesus appears before the gathered disciples who are in hiding, they do not recognize him until he shows them his wounds and eats with them (Luke 24:36-43). Again, the continuity of Jesus' concrete actions in both the past and the present—showing the wounds of the Crucifixion, touching his flesh, and eating—reveal him as the resurrected Christ. The Resurrection affirms God's continual activity in history and bears the promise that neither sin nor death can halt God's work. In spite of vanquishment, torture, marginalization, and oppression, God's love will triumph in the end; and those who are trivialized, rejected, humiliated, and murdered in anonymity by the machinations of the powerful will not be forgotten by God. Who Jesus was to the disciples was not revealed only through his words but also through his actions and character. It was not just the "what" of Jesus' life and message (the content), but the "how" that revealed him as the Christ.

Jesus is not present only in religious rituals and acts of compassion. He is also present in the ordinary activities that are necessary for the preservation of life. The Gospels portray him as being active in everyday events such as eating, cooking, and speaking with his disciples after the Resurrection. In these acts, Jesus is concretely present in their midst.

Jesus' ascension does not negate Jesus' continual presence in the world. Jesus continues to work in all our lives through the presence of the Holy Spirit. In Matthew's Gospel, we are assured of Jesus' continual presence in our midst (Matt. 28:20). The Ascension narratives are not intended to deny Jesus' presence with us, but to affirm Jesus' heavenly power.[33] The Ascension ruptures the distance and opposition between Jesus' immanence and God's transcendence. Jesus, God with us, is also present in heaven. Jesus' humanity, not just his spirit, is present in heaven as on earth. Thus Jesus not only joins humanity and divinity in himself but also immanence and transcendence.[34]

Death transforms Jesus, but he does not cease to act nor to have an impact on those who continue to live. On the contrary, he continues to ensure that both their spiritual and bodily needs are met by sharing with them, eating with them, and even preparing food for them (John 21:1-14). Jesus is present in the everyday activities that are necessary to sustain life. And today it is difficult for Christians to deny that he continues to act in a recognizable fashion and in concrete ways in and through our lives.

God's activity does not cease, nor is it limited to those events that occurred in Palestine almost two millennia ago. The God who acts in the Bible continues to act in history and in our lives today. Those Christians living in Latin America, for whom Jesus is not a transcendent reality removed from daily experience, recognize this continual activity. Jesus continues to be experienced by them as actively present to the masses, through the work of living saints, in cultural symbols, at sacred places, and in those who act out love and compassion on behalf of others.[35]

In spite of the borders, whether political or generational, these same ways of experiencing Jesus are also present in Hispanic cultures in the United States. The inescapable heritage of Latin America still flows in our veins, bringing with it the life-giving presence of Jesus Christ. In our language and our cultures Jesus continues to be immediately present and active in our lives. Through him we are able to subsist, hope, and work to bring forth change. Thus the requirements for doing Christology within a Hispanic context require a rediscovery and a reaffirmation of how Christ is actively present in our history today.

VERBO, PRAXIS, AND HISPANIC CULTURE

The power and imagery unleashed by thinking about Jesus and God as a verb are extraordinary, creating a different "feel" to the way the Christian church envisions God. They are integral to Latin American and Hispanic Christianity alike. Whether one stands on one side of the border or the other, an active God who works to change the human condition is necessary for all who suffer from injustice, oppression, and marginalization. An active God is also necessary for the entire church and Christian community's opening the door to change, action, and the transformation of this world.

The God that does not change or feel becomes a mere idol who is impotent, dead, and deaf to the cries of the people. Unfortunately, the churches who serve this God also become impotent, dead, and deaf to the cries of humanity, and unable to respond to the needs of human suffering and pain. Hispanic Americans and others living in the shadow of domination, oppression, racism, and social injustice demand change and action from God and from the church. Without change, there is no hope for the powerless and the afflicted. Without change, only those who rule in comfort are satisfied.

However, the ideals of liberation theologies need not be limited to the Third World, Latin America, and marginalized groups in North American society. In our fragmented society, plagued by violence, greed, and hatred, there is a need for the Christian church to act not merely at the individual level but on a larger, societal scale. When churches spiritualize and privatize faith, they become trapped in inaction and eventually become of little consequence to society. Hispanic theologians point out that in the Scriptures, God works through the particular actions of people, and ultimately in the particular actions of one person, Jesus Christ, to bring salvation to everyone.[36] When God works through concrete circumstances and persons to bring forth change on a global scale, it is difficult to see how some churches and individuals today can claim that faith is solely a private and spiritual affair. The church as a whole needs to recover its concrete social locus and become an active part of our society. In other words, the church needs to recover its faith in the God who acts in human history. It needs to rediscover the power of the living Verb.

Rethinking the Attributes

Traditional theological language does not always resonate with the faith of the people, but it should. Most people, including Hispanics, see God as active in their lives. For them, God is not a noun. God is the living verb—a God of action. As I have discussed above, the Bible describes God as being active in history. Yet traditional theological language refers to God in terms of substance, immutability, and impassibility. These static philosophical categories evoke images of a static and unchanging God that are useless to a people who demand hope for tomorrow.

Abstract philosophical language, used in some academic theological circles, conjures images of an uncaring, unfeeling, and distant God that is alien to most people. It is doubtful that the people who go to church to pray and worship, whether they are Hispanic or not, ever pray to an immutable and impassible "God." Most of them probably don't even know what those words mean. Instead, the people in our churches pray to and worship the living God in whom their hope resides.

When some theologians speak of an immutable god who does not change, it brings little hope to those who live in poverty. Rich people do not want things to change, but the poor want things to be different. If God were immutable, then our prayers would fall upon the deaf ears of such a changeless "God." What difference would a prayer make if God does not change?

A changeless (immutable) god is an abstraction. It is a logical necessity once believed to be required by certain tenets of Greek philosophy. According to this line of thought, if God is perfect, then God cannot change. If you are already perfect, any change would be toward imperfection—God could change only for the worse. As a result, some people find a certain sense of comfort in a perfect god who does not change. However, an immutable god is a dead god. Life by its very definition requires growth and change. Like the people of Nineveh in the book of Jonah, we want our prayer to turn away God's wrath. Although we may not want God's character and love toward us to change, we definitely want a God who hears our prayers. We want to make a difference to God.

An impassible god who does not feel emotions is protected from the passions of humanity. Unlike the Greek gods who acted out of anger, jealousy, and hate, we want our god to be unmoved by emotions and whims. But such a god is a mere machine who cannot love. We may want God to be a certain type of god; but when we fashion a god out of our logic and desires, we create a dead idol that replaces the living God. A living God loves the world, and love is certainly not impassible and unmoved. If anything, the God who concretely acts out of love for humanity in the Scriptures is a God who is immutable in love, never changing the nature or steadfastness of that love for us. And if God is impassible, it is only in his impassibility for hatred—a hatred that can never enter or participate in God's love. Thus, the fullness of God's love encounters the horror of our sinfulness as mercy for the victims of our sins and as judgment for those who sin by perpetuating oppression, hatred, and murder.

In love, God's transcendence does not negate God's immanence in any respect. Most Hispanics believe in an immanent God who is accessible to them and who stands with them. But they also believe in a transcendent God who can empower them. The God of the Incarnation is also the God of the Resurrection and of the Ascension. Only through such a God can we ever hope to overcome the cross of suffering, humiliation, and death that we bear. The same God who stands with us and dies with us must also be able to rise with us. God's ability to transcend suffering, oppression, evil, and death is our only source of hope. But this does not mean that God does not participate in them. God does not circumvent suffering and death; God overcomes them. God is not transcendent because God stands outside of our world, watching us from a distance. Rather, God is transcendent because God is able to overcome the powers of evil and death. Likewise, God empowers us to overcome these powers not through dominance, but through love. God's love transcends the powers of evil not by force, but by the creation of new possibilities for life and goodness in spite of death and evil. God's transcendence does not negate God's immanence but completes it by making possible the impossible.[37]

When we fashion our images and concepts of God, we are always faced with the temptation of idolatry. Our good intentions and fabrications for protecting God often trick us into fashioning intellectual idols.[38] The gods created by some philosophers and theologians are ultimately intellectual idols and dead gods that have little to do with the living realities of our world.[39] They are abstractions, taken out of the context of a living God who acts in our history, reducing God to static notions. In a sense, they crucify the living God. They nail God down to their definitions. They hold God captive, nailed to a structure built by human hands, rendered immobile and subjected to our control. When we limit God to these abstractions, we murder God. We effectively kill the living

God of faith, nailed to the cross of our intellectual qualifiers and logical necessities. We keep God from being God.

Theologies are meant to empower us to live as God intended. Theology should liberate and empower people to live their faith. It should capture their imagination and foster in them a vision of hope for the future. Unfortunately, much of our theological language, often overly laden with technical and philosophical jargon, can speak to very few people beyond the academy. Although such technical language is necessary and appropriate for enhancing certain aspects of our theology in its theoretical and critical functions, it should not be the sole expression of all our theological reflections. Nor can we allow it to limit or define all of our theological thoughts. Rather than forcing God into the narrowness of a few philosophical creations, we should let our experience with God guide our thoughts and expand our understanding, philosophy, and language. Instead of developing the divine attributes through abstractions and negations, theology needs to affirm who God is. Rather than defining God in terms of what God is not—infinite, infallible, immutable, impassible—we should try to understand who God is by what God does.

CONJUGATING GOD

Most of our traditional christological language in the West was shaped by the cultures in which it was born. It used the philosophical categories available to the church in its infancy, categories that came primarily from Greek philosophy. In addition, the subtleties of the Greek and Latin languages imbued our Christology with terms that lent a hand in shaping and defining Christology for years to come. In time, some of these subtleties were lost through translation and through the influence of other philosophical tools that became available to the church. But traditions tend to persist. What people today think of certain christological terms such as *person, substance, essence,* and *change* are quite different from what people thought when Christology first began to take shape. If translation caused christological conflicts between those who spoke Greek and those who spoke Latin in the third and fourth centuries, imagine how much more it can affect us today. Thus, most Christologies are laden with confusing terms and ancient language that fail to speak as clearly to those of us who are living at the dawn of a new millennium as they may have to those who first used such terms.

Spanish has a unique advantage in developing its christological language. Not only does it allow one to speak about Jesus freely without fear of being sacrilegious, but it also allows one to speak about Jesus and God through the active imagery conveyed in a verb. This does not mean that Hispanics who speak Spanish are better at developing active Christologies, or that they are necessarily and consciously aware of the active dimensions provided in their christological language. What it does mean is that Spanish opens the door for creating different ways of speaking and thinking about Jesus and God that are beneficial for the entire Christian church.

The connection between Jesus and the image of a verb opens the door to more than just active images. Verbs express actions, but they also express commands, states of being, relationships, aspirations, and expectations. Unlike nouns, which name, and adjectives, which qualify, verbs perform. Verbs also connect subjects with their objects, and in Spanish, they can bear their subjects through their conjugation. For example, "I love" in Spanish is *amo* and "you love" is *amas*, and so forth. Thus a single verb can convey a subject in action, and in some cases, such as the imperative, with the addition of a suffix they can even convey their object.

Naturally, referring to Christ as God's incarnate Verb does not necessarily imply a connection between the grammar of a verb and Jesus of Nazareth. But it enables us to think of alternative images and possibilities for doing Christology. It opens our minds to thinking about God as active and relational. Just as a verb actively binds the subject and the object in a sentence, Jesus binds us in God's love—a theme that pervades John's Gospel and its use of *logos*.[40] Thus, speaking about Jesus and God as verbs enhances the possibilities for our christological language, forcing us to rethink how we speak about God.

Rethinking God and Jesus in terms of a verb rather than as a noun shifts Christology away from its classical substance-oriented language—a shift present in many contemporary theologies. Jesus' relationship to God is no longer conceived of through a substantial identity. Rather, Jesus embodies God's act toward humanity, thus providing an identity of activity.[41] In other words, Jesus' actions are

God's actions and vice versa. This does not mean that in Jesus there is just one divine energy or action.[42] Rather, it means that the human actions of Jesus correspond to the divine actions of God, and God's divine activity becomes manifest through the divine-human Jesus. The two—divinity and humanity—coincide, and in this manner God's divine activity also can be present in our human activities as we come to embody God's continual activity in history. This is evident in the Resurrection. Jesus, God incarnate, rises from the dead, while at the same time God raises him from the dead. In the Resurrection, God's act coincides with Jesus' act, with both serving as symbols for God's activity and Christ's own act.[43]

Jesus reveals God's love to humanity through his actions, which encompass his ministry, his miracles, his struggle against death and oppression, his passion, his death, and his resurrection. Thus Jesus' divinity resides in his activity, which conforms and corresponds to God's own activity in humanity.[44] In this sense, Jesus fully actualizes the image of God (*logos*/verb) that is inherent in humanity and brings it to fruition, revealing what is possible for all.[45]

When we place the emphasis of Christology on Jesus' activity rather than on his divine being, Christology changes. It changes by uniting two of the traditional christological questions: the work and the person of Jesus. Rather than understanding his work separately or as the result of who he is, his work is ultimately what reveals his being. Thus, the person of Jesus cannot be separated from his work. On the contrary, what he does reveals who he is.

Traditionally, Christology defines who Jesus is in terms of a substance, an underlying reality that makes him who he is. Thus the relationship of his divinity to his humanity is that of two different substances, divine and human, coexisting in one individual. Yet these definitions inevitably are just conjectures and philosophical elaborations. Instead, Christology and theology must move beyond their attempts at defining who God is—outlining what limits God—and move toward discerning what God does. God's actions define who God is for us and reveal God's being in ways that we might never imagine. To move beyond and to leave behind the static categories of substances requires us to approach the nature of Christ through the dynamic activity of God in history—as many contemporary theologians have done.[46] As a result, Christology is transformed into a Christopraxis, where the focus shifts to what Jesus does and continues to do in human history.[47]

Ultimately, theology and Christology will have to move beyond traditional ontological concerns, with their quest for being and its structures, toward ontopraxis—active being. Just as liberation theologies have shifted their concern from orthodoxy (right belief) to orthopraxis (right action), so must we shift our christological concerns from ontology (the structure of being) to ontopraxis (the act of being).

Developing a theological ontopraxis requires that we understand God's being in terms of God's actions. It also requires that we give careful attention to how God acts. Furthermore, it requires a reconstruction of theology and Christology in terms of God's activity, rather than in terms of the traditional divine attributes of negation or analogy of being. It also requires that theology today be done not just by being attentive to where we once encountered God's work—the Exodus, the Incarnation, the cross, and the Resurrection—but also by being attentive to where God continues to work today.

Such a reformulation of Christology and theology has serious implications for Christian faith and practice. It requires the church to pay close attention to the active presence of God in human history and society. Rather than understanding itself as bearing God to the world, the church must be willing to discern God's presence in the world and to follow to wherever God leads, for there is where the church truly should be.

In today's world, as in the Scriptures, the active presence of God requires us to look for God in the gutter, in the dark recesses of our cities, in the marginalized, in the poor, and in the victims of oppression. It also requires that Christians seek to embody the presence of the resurrected Christ in their communities and in their world by becoming active vehicles of God's love in concrete ways. In other words, we, like Jesus, must be willing to go beyond the proclamation of God's kingdom and take active steps to make it a concrete reality in our midst.

— 5 —

LOVE ENACTED

In Miami's Little Havana neighborhood, I was forced to confront the realities of inner-city life as friends and neighbors were lured into the dark embrace of drug addiction and crime. The violence of inner-city life was always just a few doorsteps away, and in spite of my parents' attempts to shield me from its harsh reality, it was hard to ignore the gunshots often heard at night. I still vividly remember the Halloween night when our next-door neighbor's house was fire-bombed, the man who was shot to death down the street, and the blood on the sidewalks.

Even in school it was difficult to escape the violence of inner-city life. Before I made it to high school, I had already been stabbed in the hand during a fight and played Russian roulette with classmates. I was lucky. Some of my classmates were not. One left school and turned to prostitution. Her lifeless body was found a year later. Others became drug dealers and addicts. With so many young lives around me swallowed by violence and vice, it is difficult for me to imagine how I escaped that cycle of violence.

Yet inner-city life is often filled with ambiguities. Yes, there was violence, vice, and crime in my *barrio*. But there was also abundant grace. We watched out for our neighbors whenever we could and helped each other as we were able. At night, families would gather together on their porches to play dominoes and talk while sipping lemonade. The elderly would watch the children, entertaining them with stories, and the children would help them with their chores. People in the *barrio* did not just live next to each other, they lived as a community.

Within the sanctuaries of our respective communities, Hispanics find a sense of belonging, empowerment, validation, and encouragement.[1] While poverty and disillusionment often breed violence and despair in our *barrios,* our communities are still central to our lives, establishing vital connections to our languages, cultures, and religions. Without these connections we feel estranged, adrift, and ungrounded. Thus, in spite of the fragmentation our communities suffer due to poverty, violence, and modernization, we still struggle to forge a sense of community out of the remnants. Hispanic communities often transcend geographical boundaries and extend our notions of a family beyond our blood relatives to include members of our communities.[2] As a result, our communities include people who may not live in our *barrio* but who provide these vital connections that are essential for our identity.

For Hispanic theologians, our communities are essential to our theological reflection. Unlike many academics, Hispanic theologians are not detached observers, but advocates, servants, and vital parts of their communities. Even our methodology affirms our sense of community, forming our theology through an ongoing dialogue amongst ourselves and with our communities. Thus, we provide encouragement to one another and jointly fashion a theology that considers the voices of others in our communities.[3]

LOVE ENACTED AND THE COMMUNITY OF FAITH

That churches play a central role in our communities is evidenced by the names and layouts of communities in Spanish-speaking regions.[4] One only needs to look at the names of some of the cities in the southwestern United States to see the remnants of this legacy. Cities with names such as Los Angeles (The Angels) and Santa Fe (Holy Faith) and the countless cities named after saints demonstrate how central faith is to our communities. These cities were often built around a mission or church that bore the same name—a testament to the centrality of faith in the early days of these communities.

Although a particular church may no longer be at the geographical and spiritual center of those communities, local churches still are an integral focal point in the *barrio's* sense of community. Through our churches we find hope and encouragement, even when they are no longer geographically at the center of our community. In places without an actual *barrio*, Hispanic churches serve as a central location for the Hispanic community, especially when the Hispanic population is scattered throughout the city, as is usually the case.

As I grew up in the *barrio*, my local church was a saving grace. Through its programs and services I found an alternative to the despair and violence of the streets. Within its doors I found friends and mentors. I also found a refuge and a source of strength. At church we spoke, sang, and prayed in Spanish. Throughout the years my church allowed me to retain a tie to my culture that was not always present outside my neighborhood. But more important, my church provided me with another community that was essential for my survival—a community of faith. My church, like any other, was not perfect. There were saints and there were sinners. Sometimes many of us were both saints and sinners. Yet these very human saints in my community often enacted God's love in surprising ways, making God real to me. On those occasions, Jesus was truly present in this community of faith, not in the names of the people, but in their love, spirit, and words.

So far the four questions guiding my inquiry into Christology from a Hispanic perspective have yielded the following conclusions: First, *what* Jesus of Nazareth reveals throughout his life is God's love for humanity. Second, God's incarnate presence in Jesus also reveals *where* and *when* God is present. We find God present in humanity, and, specifically, we find God present in humanity when we suffer and when we act out of love for others. Third, *how* God is present in Jesus of Nazareth is through his actions—we know who Jesus is by what he does. However, there are still two questions that remain: *Who* is Jesus of Nazareth and the God whom Jesus reveals to us through his actions, and *why* is God present in Jesus' life?

In a sense, these two questions must be taken together, for who God is also tells us why God comes to us in the life of Jesus of Nazareth. What Jesus reveals to us is God's love, and that in itself tells us something of who God is. Through the Incarnation and the Crucifixion, we come to understand that God is the very act of self-surrender that continually gives itself to others.[5] In other words, God's nature is love. God is love enacted. This does not mean that God is merely an abstraction that designates what we call love. On the contrary, what we call love is the abstraction. Or, simply put, love is an abstraction from God's being—a being defined not by substance, but by actions bounded in love. Without God's love it would be impossible for us to love others. God's love initiates and inaugurates in us the possibility of love. The genesis of all our loving acts and the basis of all our loving relationships is God (1 John 4:16-21). A loving person can only exist through God's gift of love.[6] Hence, God's love creates the possibility of love itself. Therefore, the answer to why God is present in Jesus is simple: it is because God loves us and desires life for us (John 3:16; Rom. 5:8).

However, the question of why God is present in Jesus also has a teleological component, meaning that it points us to the future, toward God's ultimate goal: the creation of a loving, holy community that includes both God and humanity. Our salvation comes through our reconciliation with God and through the restoration of proper relationship with God and creation, making possible the creation of new forms of community. By entering into communion with us, God inaugurates this new community and draws us into it through love.

God's love for humanity not only initiates a new form of fellowship, it also initiates a new possibility for being human that includes God's presence in our midst. The life, death, and resurrection of Jesus of Nazareth brings about this new fellowship of love that unites humanity and divinity in God's loving embrace.[7] Through this community, initiated by Jesus of Nazareth, God's love becomes enacted concretely in the world. But where is this community to be found and what form does it take? Is it just an eschatological expectation, or is it a possibility inherent in the present? How do Hispanics fit into this community, and what is the role of the church in establishing it? The answers to these questions still await us. But in the lives of Jesus' followers and in the church we see glimpses of God's kingdom and the community of faith.

FROM BABEL TO PENTECOST

In the preceding chapters I explored the role of language in Christology. I also explored how language affects and creates theological imagery, arguing the importance of language for theological reflection. However, beyond its semiotic nature language also plays another vital role in our lives. Language is essential to the establishment of a community. As a result, the role of language is central to the establishment of the community of faith.

The designation *community* implies that its members have the ability to communicate. But is communication purely linguistic in nature? As the biblical story of Babel illustrates, language has the potential to both create and fragment a community (Gen. 11:1-9). In the story of Babel, the people's common language enables them to build not only a tower but also a city. Implicit in this account is the suggestion that they are able to accomplish the building of the city and tower because they share a common language that facilitates the building of this community. However, when they cease to share a language they not only abandon the construction of the tower, they also abandon the city as well. Why does this happen? Is it merely the absence of a common language that wreaks so much havoc in this community? The story is not a parable about the importance of having a common language in order to form a community. After all, it is God who confuses the language of the people at Babel. The story of Babel illustrates something else. It helps us to see that while a common language provides a foundation for the establishment of a community, unless other common elements are present, language alone is insufficient. An inability to communicate can disperse us, effectively preventing the creation of a community, when language is the sole common denominator.

Thus, the story of Babel is about more than the confusion of languages. It is also about community, sharing, and human pride. Without diversity in our communities, we easily lose sight of our place in creation and fancy ourselves to be the definitive standard for everything. Rather than creating a living community that is open to others, we create a static absolute. Or worse, we cease to see ourselves as a part of God's creation and try to take God's place in the "heavens" as the inhabitants of Babel attempted by building their tower. On the other hand, diverse communities provide us with diverse perspectives. These perspectives enrich our dialogue and prevent us from usurping God's place in the heavens. The people of Babel do not lose their sense of community because they are unable to communicate. They never had a sense of community in the first place! Language was merely a tool being used to create their community; but because they lacked any other common ground, they were unable to deal with the diversity of languages that emerged. So because their "community" was based solely on conformity and singularity, it fell apart when their common denominator was taken away by God.

At Pentecost, the opposite occurs: God forms a true community out of diversity. Unlike Babel, where the people attempted to build a community through a common language, at Pentecost the community is built upon sharing God's spirit. Through the Holy Spirit, God affirms our diverse languages and cultures, without the imposition of one language upon everyone. The miracle of Pentecost is not the creation of a common language that everyone understands. The miracle of Pentecost is that everyone is able to hear God's word in their own tongue (Acts 2:1-11). While the "English-only" movement in the United States is currently trying to create a national community by the imposition of a single language upon everyone, Pentecost affirms our diverse languages at the creation of the Christian community.

Those of us who speak more than one language fluently know well the limits of language. Every language adds and discloses new shades of meaning, new ways of thinking, and new ways of envisioning reality. Thus, it should not surprise us that when God's word comes to us, it comes in a multiplicity of tongues, each language providing unique flavors, images, and hues to the fullness of God's word. Only when we begin to appreciate and explore the rich texture and imageries of our languages will we be able to come closer to hearing God's word in its fullness.

The stories of Babel and Pentecost are not about creating a community through the imposition of one language or one set of norms. Rather, they help us understand that a true community requires more than a mere common denominator. A true community requires an ability to bridge our differences without dissolving them. At Babel the people are confused when they begin to speak different languages, so they cease to work together. Rather than attempting to bridge their differences, they go their separate ways. At Pentecost the languages remain different, but the differences are bridged by God without being dissolved. God does not call us to eradicate our differences but to bridge them. Thus we broaden our languages and our horizons by celebrating our differences while finding common ground in God.

The community created by God on Pentecost shared in ways that went beyond language and mere communication. They shared in the life of God. According to the book of Acts, the Christian community in Jerusalem not only shared communion through the Eucharist but also shared their meals and property as needed (Acts 2:44-47). Pentecost formed a community that broke through not just the barriers of language and culture but also the barriers of wealth and social class. Whether it is through sharing our bread in communion or our struggles and hopes in life, Christ calls us to form a community not through the imposition of a single standard, but by sharing what we have and who we are with others.

SHARING IN COMMUNITY

Language provides a clue to the nature of a community in another sense. Etymologically, both *community* and *communication* share a common origin in the Latin word *communis*, from which we also get the words *common* and *communion*. At the roots of all these words is not the ability to speak, but the ability to share and to come together in unity. Even the Greek word *koinonia*, often used to describe the fellowship of the church, shares this meaning of community and communion. All of these words ultimately refer to a mutual sharing with one another. A community implies more than geographical proximity; it implies that the members of a community share something with one another.

However, they do not necessarily share just some common aspects or interests. It is the act of sharing itself that constitutes a community. Thus, a community is more than a group that holds something in common; it is also a group engaged in the act of sharing with one another. Such a community need not be reduced to a static or ontological common denominator. On the contrary, it can be composed of diverse and distinct elements that come together in their act of sharing with one another.

Traditionally, Christology refers to the sharing of divine and human attributes in the person of Jesus as the *communicatio idiomatum*—a term that comes from the same root as *community* and *communication*. According to traditional Christology, due to the *communicatio idiomatum* Jesus' human nature can partake in the characteristics of his divinity and vice versa. In both Latin and Greek, the term *idioma* means "one's own," "private," or "peculiar." From it we get the words *idiom* and *idiomatic* in English, which both refer to aspects of a language that are peculiar to a region. Hence, the *communicatio idiomatum* refers to the ability of divinity and humanity to share what is particular to each in one person.

In the person of Jesus Christ, divinity and humanity come together through a mutual sharing that does not dissolve their peculiar differences. Just as in *mestizaje* different cultures, races, and languages come together without necessarily losing their own characteristics, in Jesus humanity and divinity come together. Consequently, in Christ, God and humanity partake of one another, not only by creating the ultimate *mestizaje* but also by providing the paradigm for life on earth. Just as God comes into communion with us to form a new community, so are we to enter into communion with each other. Thus, when we live in communion with one another, we come closer to being like God. And through this communion, we inaugurate the kingdom of God.

UTOPIA AND THE KINGDOM OF GOD

Once, during a lecture in Hispanic theology, a student asked me: "What is your utopia?" In other words, she was asking me what Hispanics wanted in a utopia, or more precisely, in a perfect world. My problem in answering her question is that we, Hispanics, are living in utopia. But not in the way utopia is typically defined. For most people, utopia is an idyllic place that has a perfect political and social system, like the imaginary island in Thomas More's book by that title. Yet the jest of it is that More named the island Utopia because it did not really exist. The word *utopia* comes from the Greek and literally means "no place." So in a very literal and real sense, most Hispanics do live in utopia, for we do not have a place in this society or a land truly to call our own.

Most Hispanics live "in the hyphen," between the cultures of their original lands and that of the United States. Yet they find it quite difficult to fully belong in either culture. Our countries of origin no longer accept us as being one of them. When we visit our native lands, we are foreigners to them and they are foreigners to us. After all, we live in the United States; and that, in effect, distances us from the everyday aspects of our nations of origin, as well as from their struggles. Furthermore, many Hispanics are third- and fourth-generation Americans, with few remaining ties to the national origins of their parents and grandparents.

On the other hand, many white Anglo-Americans do not accept

us as part of their cultures either. They look at all of us as if everyone were a recent immigrant, even when some of our families have been here longer than most "American" families and even the Pilgrims. As with many other minorities, we are suspect in their eyes. Some fear that we will steal their employment, or worse. Others look down upon us as if we were inferior and unworthy to be living amongst them. Thus we are caught in between two worlds, not fully belonging to either.[8] It is in this sense that we live in a literal "utopia" because there is no place for us.

However, in being caught between two worlds lies the possibility of creating a new community that includes diversity and acceptance. Hispanics can participate and share in the distinct characteristics of the cultures they embody, just as divinity and humanity share their respective characteristics in the person of Jesus Christ. Living in a literal utopia where we have no place, we are in a position of truly creating a utopia, closer to the one More envisioned, by serving as bridges between cultures, races, and nationalities. Hispanics, like other people of mixed heritages, can serve as a bridge that allows different cultures, races, and nationalities to come together to form a new community that includes all people without dissolving their respective differences.[9]

Yet just because we are able to serve as a bridge between cultures does not mean that Hispanics will actually bring about this new community. It only means that we can do it if the conditions are right; and for the conditions to be right, there must be both a willingness on our part and an opportunity to do it. For both of these conditions to be satisfied, we must be willing to get beyond our bitterness and pain so that we may serve as instruments of reconciliation. At the same time, we must have the courage to face and resist the forces of assimilation and domination that would rather we conform to their established norms.[10]

Thus, Hispanics live in utopia in a third sense. We live in a utopia as a people who embody the hope of what is not yet a reality. We embody this hope as the possibility of creating a more inclusive future and a new community that celebrates differences in unison. But we also embody hope in another, more tragic, sense. For many Hispanics who find no place in our current society, their only hope is for a place and time that does not exist, at least not yet.[11] As a result, our hope leads us to live in a utopia of what could be if only things were different.

In some instances this hope is misplaced in gambling, alcohol, crime, and drugs, which promise a quick way to escape the harsh reality of the present.[12] Yet these apparent means of escape only lead to dead ends and hopelessness. However, there is another form of hope that longs for the transformation of the present into what it could be, not by escaping it, but by confronting it. Thus, we are called to confront and judge the present with the possibility of a future that need not remain in the future, but which can take *place* today by *giving it a place* in our lives.[13]

It is impossible to do Christology without a radical questioning of "utopia" and the role it plays in God's kingdom. A literal utopia—like situations of homelessness, illegal immigration, marginalization, and oppression—must be questioned in all its forms. People in these situations have no place to live, no place in our nation, no place in society, no place of empowerment. Those faced with these types of existence are denied a place in our world. Yet the very existence of these "utopias" should be questioned by Christology, for in Christ we encounter a God who exists in these very utopias to which we relegate each other.

In Jesus of Nazareth, God comes to us in a baby born into the "utopia" of "no place." In the Gospel of Luke, Jesus is born in a stable because there is no room for them in the inn (Luke 2:7). Literally, in the Greek, this verse says that there is no place (*ouk topos*) for them in the inn. And it is there, in the nowhere and no place of the utopias of our world that we must go, like the shepherds in the story, to find God. Thus, we must look for God in those living in the "utopias" of rejection, exclusion, and marginalization, because it is in those places and in those faces that we often find God coming to us.

Jesus, who is born under the conditions of "utopia," ministers to the outcasts—those who have no place in society. Often, Jesus too is rejected. He is rejected by the people of his own town (Luke 4:24-30) and by most of the people of his day (John 1:10-11). When he finally does come to a place, it is at Calvary and the cross (Luke 23:33). So, it is at the cross of suffering and death that we make a place for God. Hence, we also should look in those places for God.

Yet this very Jesus who cannot find a place in this world other than death promises to create a Kingdom where everyone—especially those who have no place—can have a place (Luke 14:15-24; John 14:2-3). Although God comes to us in many placeless "utopias," God's kingdom has a place for us. Thus, Christology transforms the despair of these "placeless utopias" into the expectation of a different form of utopia made manifest in God's kingdom. By taking these placeless utopias upon himself, Jesus makes a place in God's kingdom for us.

God's kingdom is a utopia because it hopes for what apparently does not have a place in our world: love, compassion, and a just society. But it also creates a place in us for the initiation of such a kingdom of love and justice. Thus, God's kingdom has the power to transform our present "placeless utopia" into a "eu-topia" (good place) where all people may find a place.[14] Although this type of "utopia" inaugurated by God's kingdom is not yet a reality, it does call upon us to bring it about so that all may have a seat at the banquet table of God, in a communion that creates a new community of love and justice.[15]

The task of forming this new community or utopia, inaugurated by God's kingdom, transcends cultural, national, and racial boundaries. Providing a place for everyone is the task of the Christian church as a whole. In Christ, we are all called to transcend the boundaries of race, gender, and nationality to create a new community that includes all in the totality of God (Gal. 3:27-28; Col. 3:10-15). Through the creation of this community, God's kingdom becomes a reality by bringing everyone into an ever-growing and more inclusive fellowship that allows us to be different, yet one. Only in such a community can all have a place. Thus, in Christ, our ministry of reconciliation extends beyond an individual relationship with God. This reconciliation charges us with the establishment of a new fellowship and community defined as the kingdom of God. But where, how, and when is God's kingdom to take place?

THY KINGDOM COME

The idea of the kingdom of God has ancient roots in the Near East and its beliefs in divine rule.[16] The people of Israel appropriated these ideas but also added their own elements of God's rule, which ruled not just over nature but also over history by the establishment of justice and righteousness.[17] In Jesus' time, many of his followers believed that the kingdom of God was political in nature, coming through the establishment of a theocracy. Some, like the Zealots, believed that it could only come through violence.[18] For them, God's kingdom had a terrestrial location and a political nature. On the other hand, others believed that its place was spiritual in nature. Some even believed that it was a religious reality or a special form of revelation that was not accessible to all.[19] For most of these people, God's kingdom was not temporal or material but spiritual.

Today, most people tend to think of God's kingdom as spiritual. They believe that God's kingdom awaits us in a different time and place, located in an eschatological future at the end of time or in a spiritual life beyond this world. Still, when we pray the Lord's Prayer, we pray "Thy Kingdom come." This, I contend, is closer than we might imagine.

When we pray the Lord's Prayer, we do not pray that we may enter God's kingdom. Nor do we pray that we might go to it. Rather, our prayers are clear about the place to which the kingdom of God comes: it comes to us. God's kingdom is not solely a spiritual or heavenly reality. It is also an earthly reality. The Incarnation affirms that in Christ, humanity and divinity coexist in unison, rejecting any dichotomy between "heaven" and "earth." Thus, it should not surprise us that God's kingdom does not mean a negation of God's good creation. Rather, God's kingdom affirms both creation and humanity in their divinely intended form.

This affirmation of creation and humanity that is inherent in the kingdom of God implies several things. First, it implies that we do not live in the world God intended for us. As a result, the kingdom of God is a tacit condemnation of the present structure of society by disclosing how things could be in contrast to how things are. The transformation of the present conditions of existence into God's kingdom does not mean that all of our present structures need to be abandoned. Rather, it means that they need to be transformed into structures hospitable to life, community, and dignity.[20]

Second, it also implies that God's kingdom has a teleological component. Knowing the possibility of its existence provides us with a vision and call to transform our world into what God intended it to be. Thus, the kingdom of God is a catalyst, a lure, and a vocation (calling) that draws us toward God's intended future on earth as it is in heaven.[21] We must reject radical extremists who call for the abandonment of this world and its structures as corrupt and unredeemable. Instead, we should work to transform the world in accordance with the image of the kingdom of God provided to us by Christ. After all, both God and the kingdom of God come to us in this place. If God works within the structures of this world to transform it, so should we.

Finally, the kingdom of God comes into our world not as an external imposition, but as an internal transformation. God does not force us to act in accordance with the Kingdom. God leads us to it. After all, we are taught to pray for the coming of the Kingdom. Thus, implicit in the Lord's Prayer is the need for our participation and assent in bringing the Kingdom into fulfillment. We must ask for it.

Usually the word *kingdom* elicits in us images of power and dominance. In traditional Christologies these images become associated with Jesus' office as king, ruling over the church and over creation.[22] Yet it also alludes to a radical questioning of power and governance. If God's kingdom is inaugurated through suffering, death, service, and love—as manifested by Jesus of Nazareth—then we need to rethink the notions of divine power and the paradigms of power invoked by those who rule and control our world. Power does not need to be conceived of in terms of coercion, dominance, and subjugation. Instead, it can be reconceived in terms of the sufficiency to share what we have with others without being threatened by them. Power, when defined in terms of God's love, does not seek to overpower others. Rather, God invites us to participate in God's ontological nature by loving and acting compassionately toward others.[23]

In a sense, the kingdom of God is already here, in us, as a possibility. But God's kingdom requires our cooperation for it to become an actual reality. The kingdom of God, initiated in the life of Jesus of Nazareth, can become incarnate in our lives as we allow God to work through us. The image of God, inherent in humanity, desires the coming of God's kingdom—creating a world where all can have a place and where all may find abundant life.[24] Most of us do desire to create a better world that affirms and nurtures life, not death. Yet we seem to be at a loss to find a way to make this utopia—this heavenly Kingdom—a reality in our world.

ON EARTH AS IT IS IN HEAVEN

Leonardo Boff, a Latin American liberation theologian, contends that Christianity is the prolongation of God's incarnational process.[25] What Boff means is that our faith is also a calling for us to continue the transforming work of Christ on earth. We are called to imitate Jesus of Nazareth in a very concrete way. We are called to be God's incarnate presence on earth. Christology ultimately should lead us to create God's kingdom on earth by enacting God's love. In this sense, we build a community on earth that participates in God's active love.

The initiation of God's kingdom on earth requires that we live in accordance with God's will. In Jesus, God exemplifies what it means to bear God's image on earth, and thus what it means for us to create the conditions of God's life on earth. Unlike our tendency toward isolation, accumulation, dominance, and self-centeredness, God's being enters into communion with the other through self-giving love. Giving of one's self to the other is the essence of love as exemplified in God's nature.[26] Through love, God accepts diversity and otherness, and shares power and life with the whole of creation.

Both the Incarnation and the Trinity exemplify how God's being is the sharing of self-giving love; both exist through concrete acts of love. In the Incarnation, God comes to us through Jesus' self-giving love and sacrifice. In Jesus, God shares with humanity the nature of divinity. At the same time humanity shares itself with God, creating a place where both humanity and divinity can coexist as one. Jesus' concrete acts of love for others reveal his divinity. But they also reveal the divine image inherent in humanity. Thus, we learn that God is being-for-others, and this being-for-others not only reveals God's nature but also what human nature should be.[27] Ultimately, through our concrete acts of love for others, we participate in God's life. By participating in God's life and in the power of God's love, God also makes a place for us within God's own being.[28] Hence, we find life in God's own life.

The Trinity also exemplifies how God's being exists as self-giving love. The Trinity symbolizes God's sharing activity as the ultimate being-for-others: a being that cannot be reduced to static substances. The Trinity keeps us from creating an idol by preventing our thoughts from becoming fixed on one definition of divinity, and it does so through diversity and sharing. If we think that God is the transcendent creator and source of life, we are right. But the Trinity forces us to acknowledge that God is also a frail and finite human being who acts out of love and compassion for others. God is someone who suffers while dying on a cross. Yet God is more. God is also the one who raises Jesus from the dead. And still, God is more. God is also the sharing of the Spirit that unites God and humanity to form a new community. Thus the Trinity models for us how things should be on earth: diverse persons acting as one by their self-sharing.[29] Just as the Trinity preserves each person's diversity, so should we. At the same time, through our self-giving, sharing, and love we still can participate in the divine life.

If God's kingdom is the creation on earth of a community that imitates God's love as being-for-others, then our task is clear. Diversity, love, sharing, and self-giving cannot be abstract concepts in our world. They must also take concrete form through our actions. As a result, we must work toward creating a system that not only tolerates but also includes and celebrates diversity. This requires the preservation of the other and their otherness. It also means that love must be more than a feeling or words that lack action. Love requires that we share more than our faith and prayers. It requires us to share our possessions and wealth with others. Love means that we cannot be satisfied with fulfilling just our own well-being and self-interests, but that we must also work toward fulfilling the well-being and interests of others.

Imagine what such a world would be like, if we were to put the welfare and interests of others before our own! We would not need to worry about our own self-interest and well-being because others would take care of them for us. Nor would we worry about our self-interest's impinging upon others, for we would have placed their interests and well-being above our own. If everyone were to live in this fashion, we would truly create God's kingdom on earth. This might seem impracticable in our world, for we cannot trust others to live in the same manner. Yet even if we cannot trust that others will act toward us in this fashion, we can always rest assured that God will take care of us. Thus, through faith the possibility of God's kingdom can become a reality as we trust in God's providence and transforming power.

God's love does not transform our reality through violence or through the forceful imposition of norms upon everyone on earth.

Rather, God's kingdom comes by doing God's will on earth. It comes through us as we enact God's love for humanity through our actions, compassion, and righteousness.[30] In the Gospels, the Kingdom appears as the initiation of a new community that transforms not just individual relationships with God, but all forms of social relationships through our participation and trust in God's love.[31] By enacting God's love for humanity and participating in God's love, we mediate God's incarnate presence in the world and initiate the new community of God on earth. Thus, as we make a place in our lives and in our society for those who have no place in the world, we also make a place for God's kingdom on earth.

However, the power of God's kingdom cannot rely solely upon human intent and action. God's love still acts through us, often in spite of us. Trusting in the transforming power of God gives us the assurance that love will prevail, reconciling all things with itself. To interpret God's love and the creation of this new community as lacking any dimension of judgment and transformation would be wrong. Love cannot exist without judgment. However, judgment does not necessarily imply damnation or retribution—neither of which stem from love. Judgment implies the discernment of value and truth in our actions and in society. God's love forces us to confront hatred, exclusion, and oppression by showing us the alternative. As a result, if we are to live in God's kingdom, a demand to act in accordance with the conditions of the kingdom is placed upon us.

By enacting and participating in God's love through our lives and in our society, we initiate and perpetuate the kingdom of God. Thus we can live in community with one another under the conditions that affirm life. On the other hand, if we continue to participate in and perpetuate the structures of sin, hatred, and oppression, then we are condemned to live under those conditions. Thus we are condemned to live subject to the conditions of alienation, hatred, and death.

CHRISTOLOGY FROM A HISPANIC PERSPECTIVE

I grew up caught between two worlds—two languages, two countries, and two cultures—never quite fitting in either. I grew up in the in-between of the borderlands, the juncture of cultures, languages, and races. We Hispanics live in the borderlands, not just geographically but also ontologically.[32] We embody the borderlands as different cultures, languages, and races converge in our lives, shaping who we are. Yet the very nature of our borderland existence helps us to better understand Christology. By living between two worlds, we bridge the chasms between races, cultures, and languages. In our lives we reveal the possibility of incongruous realities existing together. So it is not so difficult for us to accept that divinity and humanity can come together in Jesus, not as opposite realities but as jointly real. Most Hispanics do not see Christology as an attempt to reconcile divergent elements of divinity and humanity in the person of Jesus of Nazareth. Just as our languages and our cultures come together in us, so also can God's transcendence and humanity come together. The two are not polar opposites, but mutual realities held together in the person of Jesus of Nazareth.

Jesus holds a special place in Hispanic culture by making God accessible to us. We use the name of Jesus more readily in our expressions and in naming our children, not out of disrespect, but out of our sense of solidarity with Jesus. In our suffering we see Jesus suffering with us out of his compassion for humanity. In the same manner that the attributes of divinity and humanity can partake of each other's characteristics through the *communicatio idiomatum*, Jesus shares in all our suffering.[33] Hence, just as those who suffered before Jesus' time were believed to prefigure Christ's suffering, so do those who suffer today "post-figure" it.[34] Similarly, in our acts of sharing and love for others, we see Jesus working through us.

Although Jesus' immanence and presence are not limited to the Hispanic community, we have a strong awareness of it. In part, this may be due to our language and culture, both of which facilitate a sense of Jesus' sacramental presence in our lives. Our language also may reflect the sacramental nature of our cultural disposition. These characteristics of our culture may not be readily evident to all Hispanics; they are more easily observed by those of us who are fully bilingual and bicultural.

Using the lenses of bilingualism and biculturalism to examine Christology from a Hispanic perspective leads to new christological insights and paradigms that might otherwise have gone unnoticed. These lenses allow us to see that in Jesus it is possible for humanity and divinity to come together by their actions, love, and sharing. As a result, the traditional distinctions of Christology—divided between the person and the work of Christ—lose their sharp edges within this new paradigm. We know Jesus' divinity not because of a divine essence, but by his work. Even the distinctions of high and low Christologies lose their relevance, for in Jesus Christ both divinity and humanity are affirmed together and fully. As Hispanics embody different cultures, races, and languages in their existence, so does Jesus embody humanity and divinity in his life. But the embodiment of divinity cannot be limited to what occurs in Jesus' life, for in our lives we too are called to embody God's presence through our actions.

As we enact God's love for humanity, we also embody the principles of Christology. And so it is that I can declare that Jesus is my uncle, my neighbor, and a deacon in my church. Jesus is also my friend, my *carnal*, and my parishioners. And I declare it not just because they are people named Jesus, but because in them Jesus becomes real and incarnate, mediating God to me through concrete acts of compassion and love.

— Notes —

1. What's in a Name?

1. Virgilio Elizondo makes a similar point in *Galilean Journey: The Mexican-American Promise* (Maryknoll: Orbis Books, 1984), p. 27.

2. Ibid.

3. Paul Tillich indicates that experience is the medium for theology in his *Systematic Theology* (Chicago: University of Chicago Press, 1957), vol. 1, pp. 40-42.

4. Justo L. González, *Mañana: Christian Theology from a Hispanic Perspective* (Nashville: Abingdon Press, 1990), pp. 84-87.

5. Ibid. See also *Santa Biblia: The Bible Through Hispanic Eyes* (Nashville: Abingdon Press, 1996) pp. 27-30, 32, 57-58.

6. González, *Mañana*, pp. 85-86.

7. See Anthony M. Stevens-Arroyo's definition in *Discovering Latino Religion: A Comprehensive Social Science Bibliography* (New York: Bildner Center Publications, 1995), pp. 28-29.

8. See my article "Guidepost Along the Journey: Mapping North American Hispanic Theology," in *Protestantes*, David Maldonado, ed. (Nashville: Abingdon Press, 1998).

9. Ada María Isasi-Díaz argues in favor of this point as well in *En la Lucha/In the Struggle: A Hispanic Women's Liberation Theology* (Minneapolis: Fortress Press, 1993), pp. 52-54.

10. Ana Maria Diaz-Stevens emphasizes this same point in her article "In the Image and Likeness of God: Literature as Theological Reflection," in *Hispanic-Latino Theology: Challenge and Promise*, Ada María Isasi-Díaz and Fernando Segovia, eds. (Minneapolis: Fortress Press, 1996), pp. 88-91. Similarly, Ana María Pineda's article, "The Oral Tradition of a People: Forjadora de Rostro y Corazón," found in the same volume, illustrates the importance of oral tradition and the power of the spoken word in the New World, pp. 104-16.

11. While Hispanic theologians might generate their own ideas and develop their own work, we often discuss this work with others and in many cases share and incorporate each others' ideas into our work. For instance, the very fact that I am emphasizing this point of doing theology as dialogue is a product of this process. Ismael Garcia, who is at Austin Presbyterian Seminary, suggested that I emphasize this point after reading a draft of my manuscript.

12. González, *Mañana*, pp. 28-30.

13. González, *Santa Biblia*, pp. 17-21.

14. Alfred North Whitehead also argues against the pretense that any perspective can encompass the entire interrelated complex of reality that we inhabit. *Process and Reality: Corrected Edition* (New York: Free Press, 1979), p. 67.

15. Irene Lawrence supports a similar claim by looking at Augustine, Aquinas, Tillich, Ramsey, and others concerned with the role of language in theology. *Linguistics and*

Theology: The Significance of Noam Chomsky for Theological Construction (Metuchen: American Theological Library Association Monograph Series, 1980) no. 16, pp. 98-105.

16. Bauer, Walter, *Greek Lexicon* (Chicago: University of Chicago Press, 1958), pp. 477-78.

17. Charles Hartshorne, in a private conversation with the author at his home in Austin, Texas, on March 21, 1997.

18. Alfred North Whitehead writes: "Systematic theology should be accompanied by a critical understanding of the relation of linguistic expression to our deepest and more persistent intuitions." *Adventures of Ideas* (New York: Free Press, 1933, 1967), p. 163.

19. See Mark R. McMinn, et al., "The Effects of God Language on Perceived Attributes of God," *Journal of Psychology and Theology* 21 (Winter 1993), pp. 309-14.

20. González, *Santa Biblia*, p. 16. See also Ada Maria Isasi-Diaz, *Mujerista Theology: A Theology for the Twenty-first Century* (Maryknoll: Orbis Books, 1996), pp. 19-20.

21. According to Nels Anderson, "language is more than mere vocabulary, since words can be used to convey meanings of every shade and import." See "The Uses and Worth of Language," in *Studies in Multilingualism*, Nels Anderson, ed. (Leiden: E. J. Brill, 1969), p. 3. These shades of meaning change as affections and memories attach themselves to particular words or expressions.

22. See, for instance, Ludwig Wittgenstein's *Philosophical Investigations*, G. E. M. Anscombe, trans. (Oxford: Basil Blackwell, 1958), pp. 46e, § .108, pp. 191e-92e; and his *Blue and Brown Books* (New York: Harper & Row, 1965), pp. 5, 17, 25, 81.

23. Wittgenstein discusses the building blocks of language games in *On Certainty*, G. E. M. Anscombe and G. H. von Wright, eds., Denis Paul and G. E. M. Anscombe, trans. (Oxford: Basil Blackwell, 1969), pp. 10e-15e, 52e-59e, 84e. See also p. 22e on the axial nature of these foundations.

24. Ibid., p. 10e, § 61-65.

25. Ibid., pp. 1e-7e.

26. *Philosophical Investigations*, p. 15e, § .31.

27. Derrida emphasizes this point by citing Paul Valéry's writing, "In vain have [philosophers] created or transfigured certain words; they could not succeed in transmitting their inner reality. Whatever the words may be—Ideas or Dynamis or Being or Noumenon or Cogito or Ego—they are all *ciphers*, the meaning of which is determined solely by the context." *Margins of Philosophy*, Alan Bass, trans. (Chicago: University of Chicago Press, 1984), p. 292. See also *Of Grammatology*, Gayatri C. Spivak, trans. (Baltimore: Johns Hopkins University Press, 1977), pp. 50-57.

28. Alfred North Whitehead, *Modes of Thought* (New York: Free Press, 1938), p. 54.

29. González makes this point in *Santa Biblia*, p. 14.

30. Elizondo writes briefly on the intimate nature of our relationship with God and how we talk about God. *Galilean Journey*, p. 39.

31. González, in *Santa Biblia*, p. 13, speaks on how language is laden with emotions, nuances, and shades of meaning.

32. Jonathan Schooler et al., *Journal of Experimental Psychology: Learning, Memory, and Cognition* (1997).

33. Whitehead warns against mistaking linguistic abstraction for reality in *Process and Reality*, p. 8.

34. See Karl Barth on the difficulties of conveying the fullness of God through the brokenness of human language in *Church Dogmatics*, G. W. Bromiley and T. F. Torrance, eds. (Edinburgh: T. & T. Clark, 1936, 1955), I/1, pp. 149-50.

35. Virgilio Elizondo, *Guadalupe: Mother of the New Creation* (Maryknoll: Orbis Books, 1997), pp. 34-35.

36. Barth, *Church Dogmatics*, I/1, p. 57.

37. Paul Tillich, *Biblical Religion and the Search for Ultimate Reality* (Chicago: University of Chicago Press, 1955), pp. 3-5.

38. Words can create their context and create images even beyond their original intent. An awareness of these contexts is necessary for a proper theology. Charles M. Wood illustrates the power of words for creating their context in *An Invitation to Theological Study* (Valley Forge: Trinity Press International, 1994), p. 73.

39. See Howard S. Olson, "Theology as Linguistic Discipline," in *African Theological Journal* 13/2 (1984), p. 77.

40. Some older texts used *transladar* (translate).

41. John Edwards discusses the dangers of translation while affirming its necessity in *Multilingualism* (New York: Routledge, 1994), pp. 47-52.

42. Gustavo Pérez Firmat, *Life on the Hyphen: The Cuban-American Way* (Austin: University of Texas Press, 1994), p. 3.

43. Ibid.

44. *Christopher Morse, Not Every Spirit: A Dogmatics of Christian Unbelief* (Valley Forge: Trinity Press International, 1994), pp. 47-48.

45. Paul Tillich recognized the intricate connection between religion and culture and the need to prevent a dualism between them. *Theology of Culture*, Robert C. Kimball, ed. (New York: Oxford University Press, 1959), pp. 41-43.

46. Suzanne Romaine, *Bilingualism* (Oxford: Blackwell Press, 1994, 2nd ed.), pp. 112-13. Some studies indicate that bilingual children may be more sensitive to the different formal aspects of language than monolingual children, displaying more creative insights and more conceptual and symbolic flexibility.

47. See Virgilio Elizondo, *Christianity and Culture: An Introduction to Pastoral Theology and Ministry for the Bicultural Community* (Huntington: Our Sunday Visitor, Inc., 1975), pp. 154-58, and González, *Santa Biblia*, pp. 77-90.

48. Virgilio Elizondo, *The Future Is Mestizo: Life Where Cultures Meet* (Bloomington: Meyer Stone Books, 1988), p. 21.

49. Ibid., p. 84.

50. Barth, *Church Dogmatics*, I/1, pp. 41-42. See also *The Humanity of God*, T. Weiser and J. Thomas, trans. (Richmond: John Knox Press, 1960), pp. 45-46.

2. Jesus Loves Me

1. Paul Tillich also argued that revelation always occurred through concrete vehicles and could not be detached from human experience. See *Biblical Religion and the Search for Ultimate Reality* (Chicago: University of Chicago Press, 1964), pp. 3-5, and *Dynamics of Faith* (New York: Harper Torchbooks, 1958), pp. 42-47.

2. According to Orlando E. Costas, God's incarnation forces us to consider revelation as contextual, concrete, and historical. *Christ Outside the Gate: Mission Beyond Christendom* (Maryknoll: Orbis Books, 1982), pp. 5-12.

3. Karl Barth, *Church Dogmatics*, G. W. Bromiley and T. F. Torrance, eds. (Edinburgh: T. & T. Clark, 1957), II/1, p. 52.

4. Barth provides an illustration of his understanding of the conditions under which Christology and God's revelation are possible in his description of the main picture on the altar at Isenheim. In this description we can see the Father only as reflected in the human form of the Son. *Church Dogmatics*, I/2, p. 125.

5. *Church Dogmatics*, II/1, pp. 3-12.

6. Ibid., p. 150.

7. *Church Dogmatics*, I/2, pp. 150-51.

8. Orlando Espín, *The Faith of the People: Theological Reflections on Popular Catholicism* (Maryknoll: Orbis Books, 1997), p. 16.

9. Ibid., pp. 13-14.

10. Marcus J. Borg, *Jesus in Contemporary Scholarship* (Valley Forge: Trinity Press International, 1994), pp. 26, 112-16, 151-52.

11. Ibid., pp. 19-36, 97-116.

12. Schubert Ogden argues in *Is There Only One True Religion or Are There Many?* (Dallas: Southern Methodist University Press, 1992), pp. 79-86, that while Jesus represents salvation, God constitutes it.

13. Espín, *Faith of the People*, pp. 12-13.

14. Hans Urs von Balthasar proposes a similar argument in *A Theology of History* (New

York: Sheed and Ward, 2nd ed. 1963), pp. 79-80. In this text he argues that although Jesus is the standard, in the sharing of Jesus' life and spirit, others can instantiate his presence to their contemporaries through their faithfulness.

15. For instance, this is the approach chosen by Karl Barth in many of his works, although he still maintains the necessity for revelation to occur through the humanity of Jesus.

16. Justo L. González critiques the static notions of essence assumed by Chalcedon in *Mañana: Christian Theology from a Hispanic Perspective* (Nashville: Abingdon Press, 1990), p. 150.

17. Ibid., p. 151.

18. González cites a passage from Barth's *Church Dogmatics*, IV/I, p. 186, that rejects the contrast between divinity and humanity as an untenable position after the Incarnation. *Mañana*, p. 151.

19. The radical nature of this claim is not unprecedented. There is sufficient evidence in Scripture to indicate that the incarnate Christ's importance comes from the fullness of God's presence, not because of radical discontinuity with human existence. See further the discussion in Aloys Grillmeier's book *Christ in Christian Tradition: From the Apostolic Age to Chalcedon*, vol. 1, John Bowden, trans. (Atlanta: John Knox Press, 1964, 1975), pp. 24-25.

20. Jon Sobrino, *Jesus the Liberator: A Historical-Theological Reading of Jesus of Nazareth*, rev. ed., Paul Burns and Francis McDonagh, trans. (Maryknoll: Orbis Books, 1993), pp. 75-80.

21. Ibid., pp. 74-75.

22. Augustine, *On the Trinity*, 8.10.14, in *The Nicene and Post-Nicene Fathers*, First Series, vol. 3, Philip Schaff, ed. (Albany, Ore.: Ages Software, 1997), p. 232.

23. Ibid., 9.1.1, p. 234.

24. Peter Abelard, *Exposition of the Epistle to the Romans*, 2.1-3, in *A Scholastic Miscellany: Anselm to Ockham*, Eugene Fairweather, ed. and trans. (Philadelphia: Westminster Press, 1956).

25. Ismael García arrives at a similar conclusion and provides a useful interpretation of how Hispanics understand God's love in the building of community and as justice. *Dignidad: Ethics Through Hispanic Eyes* (Nashville: Abingdon Press, 1997), pp. 124-30, 143.

26. García defines the primary ethical dimension of Hispanic life in terms of care. This also becomes a possible dimension of the Hispanic's understanding of God as love. Ibid., pp. 53-64, 125.

27. García defines some of these qualities of love Hispanics experience in *Dignidad*, pp. 124-30. Some of these notions also resonate for me with the statements of Alfred North Whitehead in *Process and Reality: Corrected Edition* (New York: Free Press, 1979), pp. 342-43.

28. Vincent Brümmer provides a good argument for using love as a key conceptual model in systematic theology for understanding our relationship with God. *The Model of Love: A Study in Philosophical Theology* (Cambridge: Cambridge University Press, 1993), see pp. 3-35 for the initial development of his argument.

29. For instance, Justo González develops a Christology that defines Jesus' divinity in terms of his self-giving love for others in *Mañana*, pp. 151-54. Espín, in *Faith of the People*, pp. 14-15, also understands the entrance of God into history as being the result of God's love, revealing to us that God cared enough about us to intervene in human history.

30. Tom Driver, in the introduction to *Christ in a Changing World: Toward an Ethical Christology* (New York: Crossroad, 1981), insists that ethics should be the starting point of Christology. However, I maintain that love is the starting point of Christology because love presupposes and undergirds Christian ethics.

31. Brümmer, *The Model of Love*, p. 110.

32. Ibid., pp. 110-11.

33. Ibid., pp. 110-26.

34. Joseph Allen provides a good description and definition of *agape* love in *Love and Conflict: A Covenantal Model of Christian Ethics* (Lanham: University Press of America, 1985), pp. 60-81.

35. Brümmer, *The Model of Love*, p. 130.

36. González, *Mañana*, p. 151.

37. Ibid., pp. 152-54.

38. See Eberhard Jüngel's discussion on God as love in *God As the Mystery of the World: On the Foundation of the Theology of the Crucified One in the Dispute Between Theism and Atheism*, Darrell L. Guder, trans. (Grand Rapids, Mich.: Eerdmans, 1977, 1983), pp. 314-30.

39. Ibid., pp. 338-39. Jüngel states that in our acts of love we know God and actualize God's image.

40. Plato, "Socrates Defense (Apology)," in *The Collected Dialogues of Plato*, Edith Hamilton and Huntington Cairns, eds. (Princeton: Princeton University Press, 1961), pp. 23, 38a.

41. Robert Brown, *Analyzing Love* (Cambridge: Cambridge Press, 1987), pp. 19-23.

42. Brümmer, *The Model of Love*, p. 151.

43. See the definition in *Webster's New Universal Unabridged Dictionary* (New York: Simon & Schuster, 1983), p. 1900.

44. I am indebted to Justo González for pointing this out to me while discussing this section on the use of formal and informal pronouns with him.

45. Roberto Goizueta, *Caminemos con Jesús: Toward a Hispanic/Latino Theology of Accompaniment* (Maryknoll: Orbis Books, 1995), p. 194.

46. Gustavo Gutiérrez, *The God of Life*, Matthew J. O'Connell, trans. (Maryknoll: Orbis Books, 1989, 1991), p. xv.

47. As noted by Virgilio Elizondo in *Galilean Journey: The Mexican-American Promise* (Maryknoll: Orbis Books, 1984), pp. 50-51.

48. Ibid.

49. Ibid., pp. 54-56.

50. Abelard, *Exposition of the Epistle to the Romans*, 2.1.

51. Bernard of Clairvaux writes: "Reason and natural justice alike move me to give up myself wholly to loving Him to whom I owe all that I have and am. But faith shows me that I should love Him far more than I love myself, as I come to realize that He hath given me not my own life only, but even Himself." *On Loving God* (Albany, Ore.: Ages Digital Library, 1997), p. 20.

52. Elizondo, *Galilean Journey*, pp. 38-39.

53. Roberto Goizueta speaks of the revelatory power of human action and the sense of solidarity we experience with Jesus as seen in reenacting the passion and crucifixion of Jesus in San Fernando Cathedral in San Antonio, Texas. During the reenactment the crowds chant *"caminemos con Jesús"* (let us walk with Jesus), which illustrates the deep sense of intimacy and solidarity the people feel with the suffering of Jesus. *Caminemos con Jesús*, pp. 32-37, 103.

54. In many of the romance languages, "Christian" was indeed used as an equivalent to "humanity." Most of these languages, including Spanish, used it specifically to refer to poor, handicapped, deformed, or defenseless individuals. The intent was to indicate that despite their affliction, these people were nevertheless human beings. Interestingly enough, the English word *cretin* came from the Swiss-French version, *crestin*, although this word came to acquire a different and disparaging meaning. See John Ayto, *Dictionary of Word Origins* (New York: Arcade, 1990), p. 145.

55. Ada María Isasi-Díaz recounts the presence of Jesus in the suffering and dying of humanity as she struggled to understand the senseless murder of an infant. She identifies God's presence in the situation by affirming that Jesus was there in the child. From "Hacia una Cristología Mujerista," an article submitted to a women's journal in Chile, forwarded to me by her as an input into my work on Christology.

56. Goizueta speaks of these concrete acts of love for others as aspects of human intimacy and familial love demonstrated in our communities, in which the universal ideal of love becomes mediated by the particular acts of love directed toward concrete particular persons. *Caminemos con Jesús*, p. 195.

57. In *Jesus the Liberator*, Jon Sobrino also addressed the dangers of abstractions in reference to Christ and to love, pp. 14-15.

58. In *Mañana*, pp. 151-54, González speaks of Jesus' life as a love that continually gives of itself to others, and cites several passages that illustrate this continual self-giving. Ultimately, Gonzalez concludes that Jesus' being is defined by love as completely a being-for-others.

59. In "Hacia una Cristología Mujerista," Isasi-Díaz tells a story of Ivone Gebara's

encounter with a neighbor who tells her that Jesus has visited her. When Gebara asked her neighbor to clarify, the neighbor says that a friend has given her the money that this friend had earned that day so that she, Gebara's neighbor, could buy medicine needed for her son. In both Latin American and North American Hispanic communities, Jesus is identified with the people who sacrificially give of themselves to help others.

60. Ibid. Isasi-Díaz finds it difficult to limit Christology to the Jesus of history, who she believes is inaccessible to us today. Instead, she argues in favor of noting where Jesus can be found today, which cannot be separated from Jesus of Nazareth.

61. Augustine, *Enchiridion*, 31.117, in *The Nicene and Post-Nicene Fathers*, p. 96.

62. Augustine, *On the Trinity*, 9.1.1, p. 234.

63. For Goizueta, God is revealed in the particular and sometimes everyday "insignificant" struggles for survival and in the life-giving acts of affection to others. *Caminemos con Jesús*, pp. 195-96.

64. Abelard, *Exposition of the Epistle to the Romans*, 2.1-3.

65. For a broader discussion of God's providence empowering our ability to act, see my article "In Harm's Way: Theological Reflections on Disasters," in *Quarterly Review* (Spring 1997), pp. 1-17.

66. Ibid., p. 130.

67. Jüngel, *God As the Mystery of the World*, p. 329.

68. As a result of the notion that God's love is the source of life and the reason for our being and creation, Augustine writes that "Because God is love, we are." *On Christian Doctrine*, Sermon 1, II. This leads Eberhard Jüngel to argue that the only reason anything exists is because God is love; that is, that God's very being is love and thus directed toward the other and creative of the "other" that is the object of God's affections. *God As the Mystery of the World*, p. 223. This same notion, that God's love is the source of life, is also echoed in liberation theologies. For instance, see Gutiérrez, *The God of Life*, pp. 9-12.

69. I refer to them as "so-called pillars of the community" because I do not think that this is an accurate term. A true "pillar" is someone who supports the structure of a community, and those who usually support the community are at its base, at the very bottom. They are the undocumented immigrants who pick our fruits and the workers who toil day and night to feed us, clothe us, and pick up our mess. I doubt that the so-called pillars of our community could last long without them.

70. According to Elizondo, by accepting those whom others reject, God forces us to confront the power groups that seek to dominate the marginal. *Galilean Journey*, pp. 70-72.

71. García, *Dignidad*, pp. 17-19, 154-57.

72. Elizondo, *Galilean Journey*, p. 108.

73. Goizueta, *Caminemos con Jesús*, pp. 176-77.

74. Gutiérrez, *The God of Life*, pp. 9-16, 94.

75. Jüngel, *God as the Mystery of the World*, pp. 221-22.

76. Whitehead, *Process and Reality*, pp. 346-47.

77. Abelard, *Exposition of the Epistle to the Romans*, 2.1.

3. AND THE VERB BECAME FLESH

1. This story first appeared in my article "A New Vision: Ministry Through Hispanic Eyes" in *Apuntes* (Summer 1996).

2. A similar argument can be found in Jon Sobrino's *Jesus in Latin America* (Maryknoll: Orbis Books, 1987), pp. 41-43.

3. A good example of this provided by Kim Neve, my research assistant, is in the Magnificat, where Mary acquiesces to God's will and in a very literal way makes the Incarnation possible.

4. Similarly, Athanasius does not limit the presence of the *Logos*/Christ to the body of Jesus. The Word of God was not bound by the body, but was in everything, while remaining distinct. See "On the Incarnation" in *Christology of the Later Fathers*, Edward Hardy and

Cyril C. Richardson, eds. (Philadelphia: Westminster, 1954), pp. 70-71. Also, Calvin's Christology and the pantheism of process theologies make similar claims.

5. See Ada Maria Isasi-Díaz, *Mujerista Theology: A Theology for the Twenty-first Century* (Maryknoll: Orbis Books, 1996), pp. 174-75.

6. See Justo González, *Revolución y Encarnación* (Rio Piedras: Seminario Evangelico de Puerto Rico, 1965), p. 24.

7. Compare to Paul Tillich's use of "symbols" as concrete signs that participate in and point to a reality beyond themselves. See *Dynamics of Faith* (New York: Harper Torchbooks, 1958), pp. 41-43, and *Systematic Theology* (Chicago: University of Chicago Press, 1951), vol. 1, p. 239.

8. See my article "Doing Christology in Spanish," *Theology Today*, 54/4 (January 1998), pp. 453-63, where I present a preliminary sketch of my undertakings in this book.

9. Jon Sobrino expands the notion of the Incarnation to include the "crucified people," so that Jesus' taking on of flesh includes the taking on of all that is weak and little in the flesh of history. *Jesus in Latin America*, pp. 43, 162-63.

10. Orlando Espín also notes the graphic nature of Hispanic iconography and paintings in *The Faith of the People: Theological Reflections on Popular Catholicism* (Maryknoll: Orbis Books, 1997), p. 72.

11. While such graphic images are rare in Anglo Catholic congregations, they are common in Filipino culture, a culture also influenced by Spain.

12. While *mestizaje* and *mulatez* mean almost the same thing, a mixture of things, the word *mulato* comes from the Arabic of the Moors and tends to denote a mixture of African and Iberian people, thus making it more appropriate to denote the cultural and linguistic mix of Iberian European and Moorish African cultures.

13. Miguel de Unamuno makes this point in the article "Spanish Religion," in *The English Woman*, vol. IV (December 1909), cited also by John Mackay in *The Other Spanish Christ: A Study in the Spiritual History of Spain and South America* (New York: Macmillan, 1932), pp. 95-96.

14. The influences of Aristotle's philosophy in Islam and its emphasis on the particular over the universal might have also affected their tendency toward the concrete over the abstract.

15. Mackay, *The Other Spanish Christ*, p. 96.

16. Ibid.

17. Ibid., pp. 96-98.

18. See Roberto Goizueta's account of this ritual in *Caminemos con Jesús: Toward a Hispanic/Latino Theology of Accompaniment* (Maryknoll: Orbis Books, 1995), pp. 32-37.

19. In *Faith of the People*, Orlando Espín writes that Jesus "is prayed to as one speaks with a living person, not merely mourned or remembered as some dead hero of the past. In his passion and death he has come to be in solidarity with all those throughout history who have also innocently suffered at the hands of evildoers," p. 72.

20. Unamuno makes this argument in *Tragic Sense of Life*, J. E. Crawford Flitch, trans. (New York: Dover Publications, 1921, 1954), p. 43.

21. Jürgen Moltmann points to God's solidarity with those who are tortured in *Jesus Christ for Today's World*, Margaret Kohl, trans. (Minneapolis: Fortress Press, 1994), pp. 64-65.

22. Like Hispanic theology, Black theology also struggles with placing excessive value on the redemptive nature of suffering. For a good critique of the dangers of attributing positive value to suffering in Black theology, see Anthony Pinn's *Why, Lord? Suffering and Evil in Black Theology* (New York: Continuum, 1995), especially p. 89.

23. Unamuno makes a similar contrast in *The Agony of Christianity* (New York: Ungar Publishing Company, 1960), p. 19.

24. Ibid.

25. Ibid., pp. 20-21. Goizueta also writes of the practice of giving Mary, the *Dolorosa*, the *pesame* (condolences). *Caminemos con Jesús*, pp. 36-37.

26. González presents a good argument and example of God's sacramental presence with the poor in *Revolución y Encarnación*, pp. 35-36.

27. Unamuno, *The Agony of Christianity*, p. 20.

28. Ibid. Unamuno equates life with struggling. For him, without the struggle of deci-

sions, oppositions, suffering, and doubt, life would cease. Yet it is interesting that the notion of struggle and life also recurs in Hispanic theology, especially in the work of *mujerista* theologian Ada Maria Isasi-Díaz, who titles one of her books *En la lucha/In the Struggle*.

29. According to Jon Sobrino, we must resist forming a cult of suffering or creating a Platonic or Hegelian dialectic in which the negative suffering serves to enhance the positive values of the Resurrection. *Jesus the Liberator: A Historical-Theological Reading of Jesus of Nazareth*, rev. ed., Paul Burns and Francis McDonagh, trans. (Maryknoll: Orbis Books, 1993), p. 234.

30. Isasi-Díaz warns of this in *Mujerista Theology*, p. 129.

31. Karl Barth, *Church Dogmatics*, G. W. Bromiley and T. F. Torrance, eds. (Edinburgh: T. & T. Clark, 1956), I/2, pp. 14, 25-44. For Barth, God's objective revelation in Christ occurs in a veiled form through the flesh and blood of the Incarnation. Yet it empowers humanity to know God as an object in history that discloses God's self-definition for humanity.

32. Ibid., pp. 203-205, 257-70. Barth also understands the Holy Spirit as the subjective empowerment of humanity to accept God's revelation and to free humanity for obedience to God. This safeguards Barth from acquiescing to beliefs that humanity could attain knowledge of God on its own.

33. Ibid, pp. 209-10.

34. Gustavo Gutiérrez in *Systematic Theology: Perspectives from Liberation Theology*, Jon Sobrino and Ignacio Ellacuría, eds. (Maryknoll: Orbis Books, 1993, 1996), pp. 24-26.

35. For Christians, Jesus' resurrection validates his message and affirms his divinity. However, for most, Jesus' divinity often overshadows his humanity, leading us to view him mainly as a "heavenly" figure. See Richard Norris' introduction to *The Christological Controversy*, Richard Norris and William Rusch, eds. (Philadelphia: Fortress Press, 1980), p. 3.

36. Ibid.

37. Martin Luther, *Heidelberg Disputation*, § 19-21, in *Martin Luther's Basic Theological Writings*, Timothy F. Lull, ed. (Minneapolis: Fortress Press, 1989).

38. See Sobrino in *Jesus the Liberator*, pp. 26-27.

39. Ibid., p. 26. Sobrino cites both Archbishop Romero and Ignacio Ellacuria, both martyred, who identified the body of Christ with the suffering people.

40. Hispanic theologians expand the notion of incarnation to encompass marginalization and rejection. See the work of Virgilio Elizondo, *Galilean Journey: The Mexican-American Promise* (Maryknoll: Orbis Books, 1984), p. 92, and Fernando Segovia's article "Aliens in the Promised Land: The Manifest Destiny of U.S. Hispanic American Theology," in *Hispanic-Latino Theology: Challenge and Promise*, Ada Maria Isasi-Díaz and Fernando Segovia, eds. (Minneapolis: Fortress Press, 1996), pp. 15-17.

41. *Galilean Journey*, pp. 30-31.

42. Orlando E. Costas, *Christ Outside the Gate: Mission Beyond Christendom* (Maryknoll: Orbis Books, 1982), p. 10.

43. González makes this same point in *Desde el siglo y hasta el siglo: esbozos teológicos para el siglo XXI* (Mexico City: A. E. T. H and Ediciones STPM, 1997), p. 26.

44. Athanasius, "On the Incarnation," *Christology of the Later Fathers*, Edward R. Hardy, ed. (Philadelphia: Westminster Press, 1954), pp. 71-84.

45. Gregory of Nyssa, "Address on Religious Instruction," in *Christology of the Later Fathers*, pp. 304-306.

46. González argues that without laborers we would not survive as a society. Thus he advocates doing theology with "aching bones and dirt under the fingernails." *Mañana: Christian Theology from a Hispanic Perpective* (Nashville: Abingdon Press, 1990), p. 129.

47. *Diccionario de la Lengua Española* (Madrid: Real Academia de la Lengua Española, 1992), vol. 1, p. 820.

48. John Ayto in the *Dictionary of Word Origins* (New York: Arcade Publishing, 1990), p. 98, provides additional words that share the latin root *caro* (flesh or meat). For instance, the word *carni*val literally means "raising flesh," referring to the removal of meat during Lent. Hence, it is a time of festivities that precedes the meatless diet of Lent.

49. The connection of incarnation to *carnal* appears in several works by Hispanics. Caleb Rosado uses it in his article "The Church, the City, and the Compassionate Christ," in

Apuntes 2 (Summer 1989), p. 31. Eliseo Pérez Alvarez cites Rosado to make a similar point in "Hispanic/Latino Christology Beyond the Borders," *Teología en Conjunto: A Collaborative Hispanic-Protestant Theology*, José David Rodríguez and Loida Martell-Otero, eds. (Louisville: Westminster John Knox, 1997), p. 35.

50. See the definition in Wilfred Funk's *Word Origins: An Exploration and History of Words and Language* (New York: Wings Books, 1950, 1992), p. 285. See also *Diccionario de la Lengua Española*, vol. 1, p. 820.

51. Karl Barth makes a similar argument in his *Church Dogmatics*, I/2, pp. 159-62. However, while Barth argues for translating *egeneto* as "assumed," I prefer to use the Spanish translation *se hizo* (made himself), which I feel comes closer to the implications of *egeneto* while avoiding Docetic implications. The masculine pronoun *himself* is due to the Spanish use of gender and refers to the man Jesus, not to God.

52. Here I intend to include both genders in the reference to God's presence in human flesh, not just as a device for inclusion, but in recognition that the image of God in humanity is both male and female as indicated by Genesis.

53. González makes a similar point, adding its significance to the work of the church as going beyond feeding the soul to feed the body as well. *Revolución y Encarnación*, p. 39.

54. González compares the Eucharist to other physical signs of God's presence, asserting that God speaks to us through physical mediums of paper, ink, sound waves, and sacraments such as baptism and the Eucharist. Ibid., pp. 31-32.

55. I originally heard this argument articulated by Enrique Dussel in a lecture given at Lynchburg, Virginia.

56. Pérez Alvarez compares the blood symbolism of the Eucharist to a metaphor of life and nourishment during the process of birth. *Teología en Conjunto*, p. 36.

57. González refers to sacraments as historic moments chosen by God to come to us mediated through concrete physical forms. *Revolución y Encarnación*, pp. 31-32.

58. Eliseo Pérez Alvarez connects the spiritual and the physical dimensions of the Eucharist, reminding us that most theologians have explored the spiritual nature of the sacrament while ignoring the physical. *Teología en Conjunto*, p. 38.

59. Alfred North Whitehead refers to all life as "robbery" for it must take life to sustain itself. *Process and Reality: Corrected Edition* (New York: Free Press, 1979), p. 105.

60. In a conversation on this subject, González assured me that the different uses are indeed connected to the linguistic and political history of England.

61. Virgilio Elizondo speaks of *mestizaje* as a coming together in a reality that does not dissolve the differences of the different cultures but rather transforms them into a new reality. *The Future Is Mestizo: Life Where Cultures Meet* (Bloomington: Meyer Stone Books, 1988), p. 82.

4. God Is a Verb

1. Mary Daly, "God Is a Verb," *Ms.* 3 (December 1974), p. 97.

2. Roberto S. Goizueta provides excellent insights into the relationship between theology and praxis in *Caminemos con Jesús: Toward a Hispanic/Latino Theology of Accompaniment* (Maryknoll: Orbis Books, 1995), pp. 77-100.

3. Orlando E. Costas, "Liberation Theologies in the Americas: Common Journeys and Mutual Challenges," in *Yearning to Breathe Free: Liberation Theologies in the United States*, Mar Peter-Raoul, et al., eds. (Maryknoll: Orbis Books, 1990), p. 29. Gustavo Gutiérrez also describes liberation theology as a second-level reflection on the lived faith of the people, that is, how the people "put into practice the fundamental elements of Christian Existence." *A Theology of Liberation: History, Politics and Salvation*, rev. ed., Caridad Inda and John Eagleson, trans. (Maryknoll: Orbis Books, 1973, 1988), p. xxxiv.

4. Gutiérrez, *A Theology of Liberation*, p. xxxiv.

5. Costas, "Liberation Theologies in the Americas," pp. 31-32.

6. Ibid., pp. 31-33.

7. Goizueta argues that the liberating capacity of praxis is not the product or goal, but the

activity itself. Thus, he makes a distinction between *praxis* (acting) and *poiesis* (making), a distinction originally present in Aristotle but blurred by Marx and, in some instances, liberation theologians indebted to Marx. I concur with him. I think the action itself is the key, but the action must also carry a teleological orientation that liberates. *Caminemos con Jesús,* pp. 86-88.

8. Costas, "Liberation Theologies in the Americas," p. 43.

9. See Paul Tillich's definitions of faith and belief in *Dynamics of Faith* (New York: Harper Torchbooks, 1958), pp. 30-35.

10. Ludwig Wittgenstein stated that a belief reveals itself not by an appeal to grounds or reasons, but by the way it regulates one's life. *Wittgenstein: Lectures and Conversations: On Aesthetics, Psychology, and Religious Beliefs,* Cyril Berret, ed. (Berkeley: University of California Press, 1967), pp. 51-52.

11. Raymond E. Brown addresses this issue in the appendix of his book, *An Introduction to New Testament Christology* (New York: Paulist Press, 1994), pp. 207-10.

12. This connection between wisdom and *logos* is discussed in Aloys Grillmeier's text, *Christ in Christian Tradition: From the Apostolic Age to Chalcedon,* John Bowden, trans. (Atlanta: John Knox Press, 1965, 1975), vol. 1, pp. 28-29.

13. See Elizabeth Schüssler Fiorenza's *Jesus: Miriam's Child and Sophia's Prophet* (New York: Continuum Press, 1994), p. 147.

14. See M. J. Edward, "Justin's Logos and the Word of God," in *Journal of Early Christian Studies,* 3 (Fall 1995), p. 263.

15. See Paul S. Minear, "Logos Affiliations in Johannine Thought," in *Christology in Dialogue,* Robert F. Berkey and Sarah A. Edwards, eds. (Cleveland: Pilgrim Press, 1993), pp. 149-50.

16. Grillmeier, *Christ in Christian Tradition,* vol. 1, pp. 27-28.

17. Justin Martyr, *Dialogue with Trypho,* sections 56-63, in *The Ante-Nicene Fathers Volume 1: Apostolic Fathers,* A. Roberts and J. Donaldson, eds. (Grand Rapids, Mich.: Eerdmans, 1950), pp. 223-29. See also my dissertation, *Infinity in Finitude: The Trinity in Process Theism and Eberhard Jüngel* (University of Virginia 1994), pp. 28-32.

18. Edward, "Justin's Logos and the Word of God," pp. 261-80.

19. Ibid., pp. 273-75.

20. That is the answer provided by the translator of Tertullian's *Treatise Against Praxeas,* in *The Ante-Nicene Fathers Volume 3: Latin Christianity,* A. Roberts and J. Donaldson, eds. (Grand Rapids, Mich.: Eerdmans, 1950), p. 600, note 11.

21. Ibid., sections 5-7, pp. 134-37.

22. He makes these statements in his introductory comments to *La Biblia Vulgata Latina traducida en Español* (Valencia: Joseph and Thomas Orga, 1793), vol. 1 of the New Testament, p. xiv.

23. Felipe Scio de San Miguel, *La Biblia Vulgata.*

24. Don Felix Torres Amat, *La Sagrada Biblia nuevamente traducida al Español* (Mexico: Libreria de Galvan, 1835), vol. 16, p. 210.

25. Horst Georg Pöhlmann writes that the New Testament is not as concerned with questions about Jesus' nature as it is with what Jesus does. It is through his actions that we experience and know his being. *Abriß der Dogmatik: Ein Kompendium* (Gütersloh: Gütersloher Verlagshaus Gerd Mohn, 1973, 1990), p. 216.

26. Ibid.

27. Brown, *An Introduction to New Testament Christology,* pp. 64-65.

28. Ibid.

29. See Harold J. Recinos' account of the "hard-hitting Jesus" in *Who Comes in the Name of the Lord? Jesus at the Margins* (Nashville: Abingdon Press, 1997), pp. 48-55.

30. See Virgilio Elizondo's "Jerusalem Principle" as defined in *Galilean Journey: The Mexican-American Promise* (Maryknoll: Orbis Books, 1984), pp. 103-14.

31. Ibid. Most likely the difficulty in recognizing Jesus after the Resurrection can be attributed to his transformation, as many of the Gospels tend to indicate. Other New Testament passages also allude to this change in their references to resurrection as a transformation.

32. Probably Luke alludes to the Eucharistic meal and its revelatory role as the place where we encounter Jesus, but there is also the action itself that helps disclose Jesus to the

disciples. Although Raymond Brown puts more weight on the Eucharistic significance of the account, he mentions that the action of breaking bread also could point to Jesus' characteristic manner of doing it. *A Risen Christ in Eastertime: Essays on the Gospel Narratives of the Resurrection* (Collegeville, Minn.: Liturgical Press, 1991), pp. 49-50.

33. See John Calvin's discussion of the Ascension in light of Jesus' triple office, especially the kingly office and his exercise of power. *Institutes of the Christian Religion,* Henry Beveridge, trans. (Grand Rapids, Mich.: Eerdmans, 1989), bk. II, chap. 16, pp. 433-52.

34. Leonardo Boff argues that the Incarnation ruptures the distinction between divine transcendence and divine immanence. Thus, they are no longer contradictory, but present in one being. *El Padrenuestro: La Oración de la Liberación Integral* (Madrid: Ediciones Paulinas, 1982), pp. 9, 43.

35. Jon Sobrino speaks to how Jesus is actively present in Latin America in *Jesus the Liberator: A Historical-Theological Reading of Jesus of Nazareth,* rev. ed., Paul Burns and Francis McDonagh, trans. (Maryknoll: Orbis Books, 1993), pp. 4, 19.

36. See Virgil Elizondo, "Toward an American-Hispanic Theology of Liberation in the U.S.A.," in *Irruption of the Third World: Challenge to Theology,* Virginia Fabella and Sergio Torres, eds. (Maryknoll: Orbis Books, 1983), p. 54.

37. See my article "The Infinity of God: A New Possibility in the Thoughts of Whitehead and Jüngel," in *Encounter* 58/2 (Spring 1997), pp. 151-70. See also Eberhard Jüngel, "The Word as Possibility and Actuality," *Theological Essays,* J. B. Webster, trans. (Edinburgh: T. & T. Clark, 1989), pp. 111-16.

38. Jean-Luc Marion expands our own notions of idols to include the intellectual realm in *God Without Being: Hors Texte,* Thomas A. Carlson, trans. (Chicago: University of Chicago Press, 1991), pp. 23-52.

39. González illustrates how philosophical language about God can become barren and static idolatrous language in *Mañana: Christian Theology from a Hispanic Perspective* (Nashville: Abingdon Press, 1990), pp. 92-96.

40. Minear, "Logos Affiliations in Johannine Thought," pp. 142-56. Minear's argument connects John's use of *logos* to a link of being that unites God and creation.

41. Karl Barth refers to Jesus as God's action on humanity in *Church Dogmatics,* G. W. Bromiley and T. F. Torrance, eds. (Edinburgh: T. & T. Clark, 1936, 1955), I/1, p. 16.

42. This view is different from the seventh-century heresy of monoenergism in that it does not deny the existence of both human and divine activity. Rather, it identifies the divinity in Jesus as being in correspondence with his humanity in an identity of activity. Thus it is more of a trinitarian assertion than it is a christological assertion.

43. See Jürgen Moltmann, *The Way of Jesus Christ: Christology in Messianic Dimensions,* Margaret Kohl, trans. (San Francisco: Harper Collins, 1990), p. 248.

44. Process theologians often speak of Jesus as actualizing or corresponding to the will of the divine *logos* that guides the creative activity of the universe (Cobb) and even speak of the divine substance in terms of fields of activity (Bracken). See John B. Cobb, Jr., *Christ in a Pluralistic Age* (Philadelphia: Westminster Press, 1975), and Joseph Bracken, *Society and Spirit: A Trinitarian Cosmology* (Selinsgrove: Susquehanna University Press, 1991).

45. According to the second-century theologian Irenaeus of Lyon, Jesus not only actualizes the image of God in humanity that has been marred by sin, he also is able to restore it. *Against Heresies,* 3.18.1-2, in *The Ante-Nicene Fathers, vol. 1,* A. Roberts and J. Donaldson, eds. (Albany, Ore.: Ages Software, 1997). Interestingly enough, Irenaeus also believed that God acts directly in human history, the *logos* being the "hand" through which God acts.

46. For instance, Moltmann moves in this direction in *The Way of Jesus Christ,* as he indicates in the preface, p. xiii.

47. Ibid., pp. 41-43.

5. LOVE ENACTED

1. For example, see Elizondo's account of how his community afforded him a sense of belonging and sanctuary in *The Future Is Mestizo: Life Where Cultures Meet* (Bloomington: Meyer Stone Books, 1988), pp. 3-13.

2. Ibid., p. 5.

3. Justo González defines this type of theological methodology in *Mañana: Christian Theology from a Hispanic Perspective* (Nashville: Abingdon Press, 1990), pp. 28-30.

4. Elizabeth Conde Frazier refers to this deep sense of community and its relationship to the design of towns in the Spanish-speaking world in relation to Hispanic spirituality. "Hispanic Protestant Spirituality," in *Teología en Conjunto: A Collaborative Hispanic-Protestant Theology*, José David Rodríguez and Loida Martell-Otero, eds. (Louisville: Westminster John Knox, 1997), p. 137.

5. See Eberhard Jüngel's explanation of how this occurs in *God As the Mystery of the World: On the Foundation of the Theology of the Crucified One in the Dispute Between Atheism and Theism*, Darrell L. Guder, trans. (Edinburgh: T. & T. Clark, 1983), pp. 368-69.

6. Ibid., p. 369.

7. Ibid., pp. 356-57.

8. For example, see Virgil Elizondo's account of his own experience of being between two cultures without fitting into either. *The Future Is Mestizo*, pp. 18, 20-27.

9. Ibid., p. 84.

10. Virgilio Elizondo speaks of the need for confronting the evil of oppression found not just in those in power, but in our own people. *Galilean Journey: The Mexican-American Promise* (Maryknoll: Orbis Books, 1984), pp. 107-11.

11. González's term for this type of hope is captured in the concept of Mañana in the book of that same title, *Mañana*, p. 164.

12. Ibid.

13. Ibid.

14. Joao Batista Libânio discusses the notions of utopia in relation to the kingdom of God in liberation theology and makes reference to the possibility of an alternate etymology for utopia as *eu topos* (good place) in an article entitled "Hope, Utopia, Resurrection," in *Systematic Theology: Perspectives from Liberation Theology*, Jon Sobrino and Ignacio Ellacuría, eds. (Maryknoll: Orbis Books, 1993, 1996), pp. 279-89.

15. Jon Sobrino speaks of the power of God's kingdom to mobilize us, as well as cites Rutilio Grande's articulate description of the Eucharist as a place where all may find a place setting, in "The Central Position of the Reign of God in Liberation Theology," *Systematic Theology*, pp. 68-69.

16. See William M. Thompson, *The Jesus Debate: A Survey and Synthesis* (New York: Paulist Press, 1985), pp. 183-84.

17. Ibid.

18. Leonardo Boff makes this reference in *El padrenuestro: la oración de la liberación integral* (Madrid: Ediciones Pulinas, 1982), p. 76.

19. Ibid.

20. Dorothee Soelle, *On Earth As in Heaven: A Liberation Spirituality of Sharing*, Marc Batko, trans. (Louisville: Westminster John Knox Press, 1993), pp. 38-39.

21. Dorothee Soelle refers to the kingdom of God as a vision that helps us create the community of love. Ibid., pp. 32-33.

22. Here I am referring to John Calvin's understanding of Christ as God's anointed, which implies three offices: prophet, priest, and king. All of these, according to Calvin, were anointed by oil as an indication of their calling. In Jesus, all three are located in one person, whose work involves aspects of all three offices. For Calvin, the kingly office was spiritual in nature and spoke primarily of his rule over the church and the bestowal of power over all things in heaven and on earth. *The Institutes of the Christian Religion*, Henry Beveridge, trans. (Grand Rapids, Mich.: Eerdmans, 1986), II, 15, 1-3, pp. 426-28.

23. Leonardo Boff, *El padrenuestro*, p. 63.

24. Soelle speaks of this desire as a portion of Jesus' utopia that lives in us and calls us to do God's will. *On Earth As in Heaven*, pp. 62-63.

25. Boff, *El padrenuestro*, pp. 9-10.

26. Jüngel defines the essence of being in terms of love as existing not just for one's self but also for the other, to create a "we." *God As the Mystery of the World*, p. 391. This definition of God's being as a self-giving love also is echoed by González in *Mañana*, pp. 151-53.

27. González in *Mañana* affirms that in the being-for-others of God's love both humanity and divinity converge.

28. Jüngel, *God As the Mystery of the World*, p. 389.

29. González in *Mañana* speaks of the "economic" Trinity in a literal sense as sharing with one another, something that we are not just called to worship but also to imitate on earth, pp. 113-15.

30. See Leonardo Boff, *El padrenuestro*, p. 63. In addition, see Mortimer Arias, who argues that the kingdom of God is experienced as action in *Announcing the Reign of God: Evangelization and the Subversive Memory of Jesus* (Philadelphia: Fortress, 1984), p. 19.

31. See William Thompson's account of the kingdom of God as a new community of the divine, defined by Jesus' love and trust of God and its power to transform society as a whole. *The Jesus Debate*, pp. 185-89.

32. Elizondo alludes to the ontological nature of Hispanics as a not-being in either "world," which also implies a new being that overarches both worlds. *The Future Is Mestizo*, p. 20.

33. If Martin Luther can extend the implications of the idea of the *communicatio idiomatum* to Christ's presence in the Eucharist, it is possible that it also can be extended to explain Christ's presence in all human suffering. See, for instance, "The Babylonian Captivity of the Church," in *Martin Luther: Basic Theological Writings*, Timothy F. Lull, ed. (Minneapolis: Fortress Press, 1989), pp. 289-91.

34. Jesus' suffering was prefigured in the suffering of innocents, prophets, and anointed men and women throughout the Scriptures according to some of the early Christian writers. In the same manner, it should be possible to say that those who suffer today "post-figure" Jesus' suffering as well. See, for instance, Melito of Sardis, "A Homily of the Passover," in *The Christological Controversy*, Richard A. Norris and William Rusch, eds. (Philadelphia: Fortress Press, 1980), pp. 37-43.

BIBLIOGRAPHY

Abelard, Peter. "Exposition of the Epistle to the Romans." In *A Scholastic Miscellany: Anselm to Ockham,* edited and translated by Eugene Rathbone Fairweather. Philadelphia: Westminster Press, 1956.

Acklin, Thomas. "The Resonance in Religious Language of the Word Summoning Human Desire to Symbolic Transformation." *Bijdragen* 45 (1984): 183-205.

Aghiorgoussis, Maximos. "The Word of God in Orthodox Christianity." *Greek Orthodox Theological Review* 31 (Spring-Summer 1986): 79-103.

Aldredge-Clanton, Jann. *In Search of the Christ-Sophia: An Inclusive Christology for Liberating Christians.* Mystic, Conn.: Twenty-Third Publications, 1995.

Allen, Joseph. *Love and Conflict: A Covenantal Model of Christian Ethics.* 2nd ed. Lanham, Md: University Press of America, 1995.

Alonso Schökel, Luis. *La Palabra Inspirada: La Biblia a La Luz de La Ciencia del Lenguaje.* 3rd ed. Madrid: Ediciones Cristiandad, 1986.

Alston, William P. *Divine Nature and Human Language: Essays in Philosophical Theology.* Ithaca: Cornell University Press, 1989.

———. "Being-Itself and Talk About God." *Center Journal* 3/3 (Summer 1984): 9-25.

Anderson, Nels. "The Uses and Worth of Language." In *Studies in Multilingualism,* edited by Nels Anderson, 1-10. Leiden: E. J. Brill, 1969.

Anderson, Ray S. "The Incarnation of God in Feminist Christology: A Theological Critique." In *Speaking the Christian God: The Holy Trinity and the Challenge of Feminism,* edited by Alvin F. Kimel, Jr., 288-312. Grand Rapids, Mich.: Eerdmans, 1992.

Aranda, Antonio. "La Cuestion Teológica de la Encarnación del Verbo: Reflectura de Tres Posiciones Caracteristicas." *Scripta Theologica* 25 (Jan.-Apr. 1993): 49-94.

Arias, Mortimer. *Announcing the Reign of God: Evangelization and the Subversive Memory of Jesus.* Philadelphia: Fortress Press, 1984.

Arndt, William and F. Wilbur Gingrich. *A Greek-English Lexicon of the New Testament and Other Early Christian Literature.* Translated and adapted from the 5th ed. of Walter Bauer's work, revised and augmented by F. Wilbur Gingrich and Frederick W. Danker. 2nd ed. Chicago: University of Chicago Press, 1979.

Ashton, John. "The Transformation of Wisdom: A Study of the Prologue of John's Gospel." *New Testament Studies* 32 (Apr. 1986): 161-86.

Athanasius. "On the Incarnation of the Word." In *Christology of the Later Fathers,* edited by Edward Hardy and Cyril C. Richardson, 55-110. Philadelphia: Westminster Press, 1954.

Augustine. *Enchiridion.* In *The Nicene and Post-Nicene Fathers, first Series, vol. 3, edited by Philip Schaff. Albany, Ore.: Ages Software, 1997.*

——. *On Christian Doctrine.* In *The Nicene and Post-Nicene Fathers,* first Series, vol. 3, edited by Philip Schaff. Albany, Ore.: Ages Software, 1997.

——. *On the Trinity.* In *The Nicene and Post-Nicene Fathers,* first Series, vol. 3, edited by Philip Schaff. Albany, Ore.: Ages Software, 1997.

Ayto, John. *Dictionary of Word Origins.* 1st U.S. ed. New York: Arcade Publishing, 1991.

Balentine, Samuel E. and John Barton. *Language, Theology and the Bible: Essays in Honour of James Barr.* Oxford: Clarendon Press and New York: Oxford University Press, 1994.

Banuelas, Arturo J., ed. *Mestizo Christianity: Theology from the Latino Perspective.* New York: Orbis Books, 1995.

——. "U.S. Hispanic Theology." *Missiology* 20 (Apr. 1992): 275-300.

Barrios, Luis. "An Hispanic/Latino(a) Agenda for the Church." *The Witness* 77 (Dec. 1994): 29-30, 32.

Barth, Karl. *Church Dogmatics. Vol. I.1: The Doctrine of the Word of God.* 2nd ed. Edited by G. W. Bromiley and T. F. Torrance. Translated by G. W. Bromiley. Edinburgh: T. & T. Clark, 1975.

——. *Church Dogmatics. Vol. I.2: The Doctrine of the Word of God.* Edited by G. W. Bromiley and T. F. Torrance. Translated by G. T. Thomson and Harold Knight. Edinburgh: T. & T. Clark, 1956.

——. *Church Dogmatics. Vol. II.1: The Doctrine of God.* Edited by G. W. Bromiley and T. F. Torrance. Translated by T. H. L. Parker et al. Edinburgh: T. & T. Clark, 1957.

——. *Church Dogmatics. Vol. II.2: The Doctrine of God.* Edited by G. W. Bromiley and T. F. Torrance. Translated by G. W. Bromiley et al. Edinburgh: T. & T. Clark, 1957.

——. *The Humanity of God.* Translated by T. Weiser and J. Thomas. Richmond: John Knox Press, 1960

Bean, Heather Ann Ackley. "Eating God: Beyond a Cannibalizing Christology." *Process Studies* 22 (Summer 1993): 93-106.

Berkey, Robert F. and Sarah A. Edwards, eds. *Christology in Dialogue.* Cleveland: Pilgrim Press, 1993.

Bernard of Clairvaux. *On Loving God.* Albany, Ore.: Ages Digital Library, 1997

La Biblia Vulgula Latina Traducida en Espanol. Valencia: Joseph and Thomas Orga, 1793.

Boff, Leonardo. *El Padrenuestro: La Oración de la Liberación Integral.* Madrid: Ediciones Paulinas, 1982.

Borg, Marcus J. *Jesus in Contemporary Scholarship.* Valley Forge, Pa.: Trinity Press International, 1994.

Borgen, Peder. "Creation, Logos and the Son: Observations on John 1:1-18 and 5:17-18." *Ex Auditu* 3 (1987): 88-97.

Bracken, Joseph. *Society and Spirit: A Trinitarian Cosmology.* Selinsgrove: Susquehanna University Press, 1991.

Brandimonte, Maria A., Jonathan Schooler, and Patrizia Gabbino. "Attenuating Verbal Overshadowing Through Color Retrieval Cues." *Journal of Experimental Psychology: Learning, Memory, and Cognition* 23 (1997): 915-31.

Brown, David and Ann Loades. *Christ, the Sacramental Word*. London: SPCK, 1996.

Brown, Raymond E. *An Introduction to New Testament Christology*. New York: Paulist Press, 1994.

————. *A Risen Christ in Eastertime: Essays on the Gospel Narratives of the Resurrection*. Collegeville, Minn.: Liturgical Press, 1991.

Brown, Robert. *Analyzing Love*. Cambridge: Cambridge University Press, 1987.

Brümmer, Vincent. *The Model of Love: A Study in Philosophical Theology*. Cambridge: Cambridge University Press, 1993.

Calvin, John. *Institutes of the Christian Religion*. Translated by Henry Beveridge. Grand Rapids, Mich.: Eerdmans, 1989.

Carmody, John. "The Biblical Foundation and Conclusion of Lonergan's *De Verbo Incarnato*." *Andover Newton Quarterly* 15 (Nov. 1974): 124-36.

Chopp, Rebecca S. *The Power to Speak: Feminism, Language, God*. New York: Crossroad, 1989.

Cobb, John B. *Christ in a Pluralistic Age*. Philadelphia: Westminster Press, 1975.

Conde-Frazier, Elizabeth. "Hispanic Protestant Spirituality." In *Teología en Conjunto: A Collaborative Hispanic-Protestant Theology*, edited by José David Rodríguez and Loida Martell-Otero, 125-45. Louisville: Westminster John Knox Press, 1997.

Cook, A. William. "The Power and the Powerless: The Pastoral Vocation of the Hispanic Church in the U.S.A." *Evangelical Review of Theology* 9 (Apr. 1985): 156-65.

Cook, Michael L. "Jesus from the Other Side of History: Christology in Latin America." *Theological Studies* 44 (June 1983): 258-87.

Costas, Orlando E. "Hispanic Theology in North America." In *Struggles for Solidarity: Liberation Theologies in Tension*, edited by Lorine M. Getz and Ruy O. Costa, 63-74. Minneapolis: Fortress Press, 1992.

————. "Liberation Theologies in the Americas: Common Journeys and Mutual Challenges." In *Yearning to Breathe Free: Liberation Theologies in the United States*, edited by Mar Peter-Raoul, Linda Rennie Forcey, and Robert Frederick Hunter, Jr., 28-44. Maryknoll: Orbis Books, 1990.

————. *Christ Outside the Gate: Mission Beyond Christendom*. Maryknoll: Orbis Books, 1982.

Crowley, Paul G. "Technology, Truth and Language: The Crisis of Theological Discourse." *Heythrop Journal* 32 (July 1991): 323-39.

Cunningham, David S. *Faithful Persuasion: In Aid of a Rhetoric of Christian Theology*. Notre Dame: University of Notre Dame Press, 1991.

Cupitt, Don. *Creation Out of Nothing*. London: SCM Press and Philadelphia: Trinity Press International, 1990.

Dalferth, Ingolf U. *Jenseits von Mythos und Logos: Die Christologische Transformation der Theologie*. Freiburg: Herder, 1993.

Daly, Mary. "God Is a Verb." *Ms.* 3 (Dec. 1974): 58-62, 96-98.

D'Aulan, Philippe. "Jesus: The Word." *Journal of Religion and Psychical Research* 17 (Jan. 1994): 53-55.

Deck, Allan Figueroa. *Frontiers of Hispanic Theology in the United States*. Maryknoll: Orbis Books, 1992.

———. "Hispanic Ministry." In *Reading the Signs of the Times: Resources for Social and Cultural Analysis*, edited by T. Howland Sanks and John A. Coleman, 168-76. New York: Paulist Press, 1993.

Deck, Allan Figueroa, Yolanda Tarango, and Timothy M. Matovina, eds. *Perspectivas: Hispanic Ministry*. Kansas City, Mo.: Sheed & Ward, 1995.

Derrida, Jacques. *Margins of Philosophy*. Translated by Alan Bass. Chicago: University of Chicago Press, 1984.

———. *Of Grammatology*. 1st U.S. ed. Translated by Gayatri Chakravorty Spivak. Baltimore: Johns Hopkins University Press, 1977.

Diaz, Ray. "La Liberación Hispana en USA." *Apuntes* 9 (Spring 1989): 13-15.

Driver, Tom F. *Christ in a Changing World: Toward an Ethical Christology*. New York: Crossroad, 1981.

Duncan, Robert L. "The Logos: From Sophocles to the Gospel of John." *Christian Scholar's Review* 9 (1979): 121-30.

Dwane, Sigqibo. "Christology and Liberation." *Journal of Theology for Southern Africa* 35 (June 1981): 29-37.

———. "Christology in the Third World." *Journal of Theology for Southern Africa* 21 (Dec. 1977): 3-12.

Edwards, M. J. "Justin's Logos and the Word of God." *Journal of Early Christian Studies* 3 (Fall 1995): 261-80.

Edwards, John R. *Multilingualism*. New York: Routledge, 1994.

Elizondo, Virgilio. *Guadalupe: Mother of the New Creation*. Maryknoll: Orbis Books, 1997.

———. *The Future Is Mestizo: Life Where Cultures Meet*. Bloomington: Meyer Stone Books, 1988.

———. *Galilean Journey: The Mexican American Promise*. Maryknoll: Orbis Books, 1984.

———. "Toward an American-Hispanic Theology of Liberation in the U.S.A." In *Irruption of the Third World: Challenge to Theology—Papers from the Fifth International Conference of the Ecumenical Association of Third World Theologians*, edited by Virginia Fabella and Sergio Torres, 50-55. Maryknoll: Orbis Books, 1983.

———. *Christianity and Culture: An Introduction to Pastoral Theology and Ministry for the Bicultural Community*. Huntington: Our Sunday Visitor, Inc., 1975.

———. "A Challenge to Theology: The Situation of Hispanic Americans." In *Catholic Theological Society of America: Proceedings of the 30th Annual Convention*, New Orleans, Louisiana, edited by L. Salm, 163-76. New York: Catholic Theological Society of America, 1975.

Erickson, Millard J. *The Word Became Flesh*. Grand Rapids, Mich.: Baker Book House, 1991.

Espín, Orlando O. *The Faith of the People: Theological Reflections on Popular Catholicism*. Maryknoll: Orbis Books, 1997.

Evans, Craig A. *Word and Glory: On the Exegetical and Theological Background of John's Prologue*. Sheffield, UK: JSOT, 1993.

Fabella, Virginia and Sergio Torres, eds. *Irruption of the Third World: Challenge to*

Theology (Papers from the Fifth International Conference of the Ecumenical Association of Third World Theologians.) Maryknoll: Orbis Books, 1983.

Fennema, David A. "John 1:18: 'God the Only Son.'" *New Testament Studies* 31 (Jan. 1985): 124-35.

Fernandez, Eduardo C. "'Reading the Bible in Spanish': U.S. Catholic Hispanic Theologians' Contribution to Systematic Theology." *Apuntes* 14 (Fall 1994): 86-90.

Fideler, David R. *Jesus Christ, Sun of God: Ancient Cosmology and Christian Symbolism.* Wheaton, Ill.: Quest Books, 1993.

Fitzpatrick, Joseph P. "A Survey of Literature on Hispanic Ministry." In *Strangers and Aliens No Longer*, part 1, edited by E. Hemrick, 63-87. Washington, D.C.: United States Catholic Conference, 1993.

Frankenberry, Nancy. "Inquiry and the Language of the Divine: A Reply to Proudfoot." *American Journal of Theology and Philosophy* 14 (Sept. 1993): 257-62.

Freed, Edwin D. "Theological Prelude to the Prologue of John's Gospel." *Scottish Journal of Theology* 32 (1979): 257-69.

Funk, Wilfred. *Word Origins: An Exploration and History of Words and Language.* New York: Wings Books, 1992.

García, Ismael. *Dignidad: Ethics Through Hispanic Eyes.* Nashville: Abingdon Press, 1997.

Garcia, Sixto J. "A Hispanic Approach to Trinitarian Theology: The Dynamics of Celebration, Reflection, and Praxis." In *We Are a People!: Initiatives in Hispanic American Theology*, edited by Roberto S. Goizueta, 107-32. Minneapolis: Fortress Press, 1992.

Gaybba, Brian. "Theological Language: Its Problematic Character." *Journal of Theology for Southern Africa* 46 (Mar. 1984): 11-19.

Gellman, Jerome I. "Religion as Language." *Religious Studies* 21 (June 1985): 159-68.

Getz, Lorine M. and Ruy O. Costa, eds. *Struggles for Solidarity: Liberation Theologies in Tension.* Minneapolis: Fortress Press, 1992.

Gibellini, Rosino, ed. *Paths of African Theology.* Maryknoll: Orbis Books, 1994.

Godfrey, Michael J. H. "Catchments for God-Talk: Karl-Josef Kuschel and Theological Language." *Pacifica* 8 (Fall 1995): 40-52.

Goizueta, Roberto. *Caminemos con Jesús: Toward a Hispanic/Latino Theology of Accompaniment.* Maryknoll: Orbis Books, 1995.

———, ed. *We Are a People!: Initiatives in Hispanic American Theology.* Minneapolis: Fortress Press, 1992.

———. "Nosostros: Toward a U.S. Hispanic Anthropology." *Listening* 27 (Winter 1992): 55-69.

González, Justo. *Desde el siglo y hasta el siglo: esbozos teológicos para el siglo XXI.* Mexico City: A.E.T.H. and Ediciones STPM, 1997.

———. *Santa Biblia: The Bible Through Hispanic Eyes.* Nashville: Abingdon Press, 1996.

———. "Redescubrimiento: Five Centuries of Hispanic American Christianity, 1492–1992." *Apuntes* 13 (Apr. 1993): 4-13.

———, ed. *Voces: Voices from the Hispanic Church.* Nashville: Abingdon Press, 1992.

————. *Mañana: Christian Theology from a Hispanic Perspective*. Nashville: Abingdon Press, 1990.

————. "The Next Ten Years [of *Apuntes* and Hispanic Theology]." *Apuntes* 10 (Winter 1990): 84-94.

————. *Revolución y Encarnación*. Rio Piedras: Seminario Evangelico de Puerto Rico, 1965.

Gooch, Paul W. *Reflections on Jesus and Socrates: Word and Silence*. New Haven: Yale University Press, 1996.

Grant, Jacquelyn. "The Power of Language and the Language of Empowerment." *Journal of Theology* 98 (1994): 5-17.

————. "Black Christology: Interpreting Aspects of the Apostolic Faith." *Mid-Stream* 24 (Oct. 1985): 366-75.

Gray, William N. "The Myth of the Word Discarnate." *Theology* 88 (Mar. 1985): 112-17.

Gregory of Nyssa. "An Address on Religious Instruction." In *Christology of the Later Fathers*, edited by Edward R. Hardy and Cyril C. Richardson, 268-325. Philadelphia: Westminster Press, 1954.

Grillmeier, Aloys. *Christ in Christian Tradition. Vol. I: From the Apostolic Age to Chalcedon*. 2nd rev. ed. Translated by John Bowden. Atlanta: John Knox Press, 1975.

Gutiérrez, Gustavo. *Systematic Theology: Perspectives from Liberation Theology*. Edited by Jon Sobrino and Ignacio Ellacuría. Maryknoll: Orbis Books, 1996.

————. *The God of Life*. Translated by Matthew J. O'Connel. Maryknoll: Orbis Books, 1991.

————. *A Theology of Liberation: History, Politics, and Salvation*. Rev. ed. Translated and edited by Caridad Inda and John Eagleson. Maryknoll: Orbis Books, 1988.

Harvey, Michael G. "Wittgenstein's Notion of 'Theology as Grammar.'" *Religious Studies* 25 (Mar. 1989): 89-103.

Hernandez, Lydia. "La Mujer Chicana and La Justicia Economica." *Apuntes* 6 (Winter 1986): 81-83.

Herzog, Frederick. *Theology of the Liberating Word*. Nashville: Abingdon Press, 1971.

Heyward, Carter. "Jesus of Nazareth/Christ of Faith: Foundations of a Reactive Christology." In *Lift Every Voice: Constructing Christian Theologies from the Underside*, edited by Susan Brooks Thistlethwaite and Mary Potter Engel, 191-200. New York: Harper & Row, 1990.

Hills, Julian Victor. "'Christ Was the Goal of the Law' ... (Rom. 10:4)." *Journal of Theological Studies* 32 (July 1986): 449-57.

Hodgson, Peter Crafts. *Jesus—Word and Presence: An Essay in Christology*. Philadelphia: Fortress Press, 1971.

Hopkins, Julie M. *Towards a Feminist Christology: Jesus of Nazareth, European Women, and the Christological Crisis*. Grand Rapids, Mich.: Eerdmans, 1995.

Inch, Morris A. "Black Christology in Historical Perspective." In *Perspectives on Evangelical Theology: Pages from the Thirtieth Annual Meeting of the Evangelical Theological Society*, edited by K. S. Kantzer and S. N. Gundry, 151-62. Grand Rapids, Mich.: Baker Book House, 1979.

Inch, Morris A. and Ronald Youngblood, eds. "The Living and Active Word of

God: Essays in Honor of Samuel J. Schultz." *Andrews University Seminary Studies* 24 (Autumn 1986): 277-80.

Irenaeus. "Against Heresies." In *Ante-Nicene Fathers,* edited by Alexander Roberts and James Donaldson, 309-567. 2nd ed. Peabody, Mass.: Hendrickson Publishers, Inc., 1995.

Isasi-Díaz, Ada Maria. *Mujerista Theology: A Theology for the Twenty-first Century.* Maryknoll: Orbis Books, 1996.

————. *Women of God, Women of the People.* St. Louis: Chalice Press, 1995.

————. " 'By the Rivers of Babylon': Exile as a Way of Life." In *Reading from This Place, vol. 1: Social Location and Biblical Interpretation in the United States,* edited by Fernando F. Segovia and Mary Ann Tolbert, 149-63. Minneapolis: Fortress Press, 1995.

————. "Mujerista Liturgies and the Struggle for Liberation." In *Liturgy and the Body,* edited by Louis Marie Chauvet and François Kabasele Lumbala, 104-11. London: SCM Press and Maryknoll: Orbis Books, 1995.

————. *En la Lucha/In the Struggle: A Hispanic Women's Liberation Theology.* Minneapolis: Fortress Press, 1993.

————. "La Palabra de Dios en Nosostras—The Word of God in Us." In *Searching the Scriptures, vol. 1: A Feminist Introduction,* edited by Elisabeth Schüssler Fiorenza, 86-97. New York: Crossroad, 1993.

————. "La Vida de Las Mujeres Hispanas: La Fuente de La Teología Mujerista." *Cristianismo y Sociedad* 31/4 (1993) and 32/1 (1994): 43-62.

————. "On the Birthing Stool: Mujerista Liturgy." In *Women at Worship: Interpretations of North American Diversity,* edited by Marjorie Procter-Smith and Janet R. Walton, 191-210. Louisville: Westminster John Knox Press, 1993.

————. "Viva La Differencia! [Hispanic and Anglo Feminist Theology]." *Journal of Feminist Studies in Religion* 8 (Fall 1992): 98-102.

————. "Mujerista Theology's Method: A Liberative Praxis, A Way of Life." *Listening* 27 (Winter 1992): 41-54.

————. "Mujeristas: A Name of Our Own." In *The Future of Liberation Theology: Essays in Honor of Gustavo Gutiérrez,* edited by Marc H. Ellis and Otto Maduro, 410-19. Maryknoll: Orbis Books, 1989.

————. *Hispanic Women: Prophetic Voice in the Church—Toward a Hispanic Women's Liberation Theology.* San Francisco: Harper & Row, 1988.

————. "La Mujer Hispana: Voz Profetica en La Iglesia de Los Estados Unidos." *Informes de Pro Nundi Vita America Latina* 28 (1982): 1-27.

————. "Hacia Una Cristologia Mujerista." Unpublished copy of an article submitted to a women's journal in Chile (1998).

Isasi-Díaz, Ada María and Fernando F. Segovia, eds. *Hispanic/Latino Theology: Challenge and Promise.* Minneapolis: Fortress Press, 1996.

Isasi-Díaz, Ada María, et al. "Mujeristas: Who We Are and What We Are About." *Journal of Feminist Studies in Religion* 8 (Spring 1992): 105-25.

Jabusch, Willard. *The Spoken Christ: Reading and Preaching the Transforming Word.* New York: Crossroad, 1990.

Jeffner, Anders. *The Study of Religious Language.* London: SCM Press, 1972.

Jimenez, Pablo A. "The Use of the Bible in Hispanic Theology." Ph.D. diss., Columbia Theological Seminary, 1994.

Journal of Hispanic/Latino Theology. Collegeville, Minn.: Liturgical Press, 1993.

Jüngel, Eberhard. "The Word as Possibility and Actuality: The Ontology of the Doctrine of Justification." In *Theological Essays,* translated by J. B. Webster, 95-123. Edinburgh: T. & T. Clark, 1989.

————. *God as the Mystery of the World: On the Foundation of the Theology of the Crucified One in the Dispute Between Theism and Atheism.* Translated by Darrell L. Guder. Grand Rapids, Mich.: Eerdmans, 1983.

Justin Martyr. "Dialogue with Trypho." In vol. 1 of *Ante-Nicene Fathers,* edited by Alexander Roberts and James Donaldson, 194-270. 2nd ed. Peabody, Mass.: Hendrickson Publishers, Inc., 1995.

Kierkegaard, Søren. *The Sickness unto Death: A Christian Psychological Exposition for Upbuilding and Awakening.* Edited and translated by Howard V. Hong and Edna H. Hong. Princeton: Princeton University Press, 1980.

Kort, Wesley A. *Bound to Differ: The Dynamics of Theological Discourses.* University Park, Pa.: Pennsylvania State University Press, 1992.

Kümmel, Werner Georg. *Vierzig Jahre Jesusforschung (1950–1990).* Weinheim: Beltz Athenäum, 1994.

LaCugna, Catherine Mowry, ed. *Freeing Theology: The Essentials of Theology in Feminist Perspective.* San Francisco: HarperSan Francisco, 1993.

Lampe, Philip E. "The Church and Hispanic Needs." In *Hispanics in the Church: Up from the Cellar,* edited by Philip E. Lampe, 158-67. San Francisco and London: Catholic Scholars Press, 1994.

Lara-Braud, Jorge. "Hispanic-Americans and the Crisis in the Nation." *Theology Today* 26 (Oct. 1969): 334-38.

Lash, Nicholas. "How Large Is a 'Language Game'?" *Theology* 87 (Jan. 1984): 19-28.

Lawrence, Irene. *Linguistics and Theology: The Significance of Noam Chomsky for Theological Construction.* Metuchen, N.J.: Scarecrow Press, 1980.

Lee, Bernard J. *Jesus and the Metaphors of God: The Christs of the New Testament.* New York: Paulist Press, 1993.

Libânio, Joao Batista. "Hope, Utopia, Resurrection." In *Systematic Theology: Perspectives from Liberation Theology (Readings from Mysterium Liberationis).* Edited by Jon Sobrino and Ignacio Ellacuría, 279-90. Maryknoll: Orbis Books, 1996.

Lilburne, Geoffrey R. "Christology: In Dialogue with Feminism." *Horizons* 11 (Spring 1984): 7-27.

Luther, Martin. "The Babylonian Captivity of the Church—Part I." In *Martin Luther's Basic Theological Writings,* edited by Timothy F. Lull, 267-313. Minneapolis: Fortress Press, 1989.

Mackay, John A. *The Other Spanish Christ: A Study in the Spiritual History of Spain and South America.* New York: Macmillan, 1933.

MacNicol, J. D. A. "Word and Deed in the New Testament." *Scottish Journal of Theology* 5 (1952): 237-48.

Macquarrie, John. "The Logic of Religious and Theological Language." *Journal of Dharma* 17 (July-Sept. 1992): 169-77.

Magalhaes, Antonio Carlos de Melo. *Christologie und Nachfolge: Eine Systematische-ökumenische Untersuchung zur Befreiungschristologie bei Leonardo Boff und Jon Sobrino.* Ammersbeck bei Hamburg: Verlag an der Lottbek, 1991.

Marion, Jean-Luc. *God Without Being: Hors-Texte.* Translated by Thomas A. Carlson. Chicago: University of Chicago Press, 1991.

Marrero, Gilberto. "Hispanic Americans and Liberation." *Church and Society* 62 (Jan.-Feb. 1972): 25-34.

Martell-Otero, Loida. "Women Doing Theology: Una Perspectiva Evangelica." *Apuntes* 14 (Fall 1994): 67-85.

McDermott, Brian O. *Word Become Flesh: Dimensions of Christology.* Collegeville, Minn.: Liturgical Press, 1993.

McFague, Sallie. *Metaphorical Theology: Models of God in Religious Language.* Philadelphia: Fortress Press, 1982.

McLeod, Mark S. "Schubert Ogden on Truth, Meaningfulness and Religious Language." *American Journal of Theology and Philosophy* 9 (Sept. 1988): 195-207.

McMaster, Belle Miller. "I Have Been Reading...Exploring Christology, Biblical Interpretation, and Ecclesiology from Womanist and Feminist Perspectives." *Church and Society* 84 (May-June 1994): 130-35.

McMinn, Mark R., et al. "The Effects of God Language on Perceived Attributes of God." *Journal of Psychology and Theology* 21 (Winter 1993): 309-14.

Mealand, David L. "Christology of the Fourth Gospel." *Scottish Journal of Theology* 31 (1978): 449-67.

Melito of Sardis. "A Homily of the Passover." In *The Christological Controversy,* edited and translated by Richard A. Norris, 33-47. Philadelphia: Fortress Press, 1980.

Meyendorff, John. "Christ as Word: Gospel and Culture." *International Review of Mission* 74 (Apr. 1985): 246-57.

Milbank, John. *The Word Made Strange: Theology, Language, Culture.* Oxford and Cambridge, Mass.: Blackwell, 1997.

Miller, Ed L. "The Johannine Origins of the Johannine Logos." *Journal of Biblical Literature* 112 (Fall 1993): 445-57.

————. "The Logos Was God." *Evangelical Quarterly* 53 (Apr.-June 1981): 65-77.

Minear, Paul S. "Logos Affiliations in Johannine Thought." In *Christology in Dialogue,* edited by Robert F. Berkey and Sarah A. Edwards, 142-56. Cleveland, Ohio: Pilgrim Press, 1993.

Mofokeng, Takatso Alfred. *The Crucified Among the Crossbearers: Towards a Black Christology.* Kampen: Uitgeversmaatschappij J. H. Kok, 1983.

Moila, M. Philip. "Christology in the Context of Oppression in South Africa." *Africa Theological Journal* 19 (1990): 223-31.

Moltmann, Jürgen. *Jesus Christ for Today's World.* Translated by Margaret Kohl. Minneapolis: Fortress Press, 1994.

————. *The Way of Jesus Christ: Christology in Messianic Dimensions.* Translated by Margaret Kohl. San Francisco: Harper & Row, 1990.

Morreall, John. "Can Theological Language Have Hidden Meaning?" *Religious Studies* 19 (Mar. 1983): 43-56.

Morse, Christopher. *Not Every Spirit: A Dogmatics of Christian Disbelief.* Valley Forge, Pa.: Trinity Press, 1994.

Murphy, George. "Cosmology and Christology." *Science and Christian Belief* 6 (Oct. 1994): 101-11.

Murphy, Larry. "African American Christian Perspectives on Christology and Incarnation." *Ex Auditu* 7 (1991): 73-82.

Nayak, G. C. "Religious Language and Religion: The Periphery and the Core." *Religious Studies and Theology* 13 (Dec. 1995): 94-102.

Nida, Eugene A. "Reina-Valera Spanish Revision of 1960." *Bible Translator* 12 (July 1961): 107-19.

Nielsen, Kai. "On Mucking Around About God: Some Methodological Animadversions." *International Journal for Philosophy of Religion* 16 (1984): 111-22.

Norris, Richard, trans. and ed. *The Christological Controversy*. Philadelphia: Fortress Press, 1980.

Odell-Scott, David W. *A Post-Patriarchal Christology*. Atlanta: Scholars Press, 1992.

Oden, Thomas C. *The Word of Life*. San Francisco: Harper & Row, 1989.

Ogden, Schubert. *Is There Only One True Religion or Are There Many?* Dallas: Southern Methodist University Press, 1992.

Olson, Howard S. "Theology as Linguistic Discipline." *Africa Theological Journal* 13 (1984): 73-82.

Omiya, Hiroshi. "The People of God as the People of the Word." *South East Asia Journal of Theology* 1/4 (1960): 9-19.

O'Neill, J. C. "The Word Did Not 'Become' Flesh." *Zeitschrift fur die Neutestamentliche Wissenschaft und die Kunde der Alteren Kirche* 82 (1991): 125-27.

Orbe, Antonio. *Hacia La Primeria Teología de La Procession del Verbo*. 2 vols. Rome: Apud aedes Universitatis Gregorianae, 1958.

———. "La Uncion del Verbo." *Theologoische Literaturzeitung* 91 (Dec. 1966): 907-15.

Pailin, David A. "The Genuinely Active God." *Modern Churchman* 27/4 (1985): 16-32.

Painter, John. "Theology, Eschatology and the Prologue of John." *Scottish Journal of Theology* 46 (1993): 27-42.

Parker, James. "The Incarnational Christology of John." *Criswell Theological Review* 3 (Fall 1988): 31-48.

Pedraja, Luis. "Guidepost along the Journey: Mapping North American Hispanic Theology." In *Protestantes*, edited by David Maldonado. Nashville: Abingdon Press, 1999.

———. "Doing Christology in Spanish." *Theology Today* 54 (Jan. 1998): 453-63.

———. "In Harm's Way: Theological Reflections on Disasters." *Quarterly Review* (Spring 1997): 1-17.

———. "The Infinity of God: A New Possibility in the Thoughts of Whitehead and Jüngel." *Encounter* 58 (Spring 1997): 151-70.

———. "A New Vision: Ministry Through Hispanic Eyes." *Apuntes* 16 (Summer 1996): 51-58.

———. "Infinity in Finitude: The Trinity in Process Theism and Eberhard Jüngel." Ph.D. diss., University of Virginia, 1994.

Pérez Alvarez, Eliseo. "In Memory of Me: Hispanic/Latino Christology Beyond Borders." In *Teología en Conjunto: A Collaborative Hispanic Protestant Theology*, edited by José David Rodríguez and Loida Martell-Otero, 33-49. Louisville: Westminster John Knox Press, 1997.

Pérez Firmat, Gustavo. *Life on the Hyphen: The Cuban-American Way*. Austin: University of Texas Press, 1994.

Peter-Raoul, Mar, Linda Rennie Forcey, and Robert Frederick Hunter, Jr., eds. *Yearning to Breathe Free: Liberation Theologies in the United States*. Maryknoll: Orbis Books, 1990.

Piar, Carlos R. *Jesus and Liberation: A Critical Analysis of the Christology of Latin American Liberation Theology.* New York: P. Lang, 1994.

Pineda, Ana María and Robert Schreiter, eds. *Dialogue Rejoined: Theology and Ministry in the United States Hispanic Reality.* Collegeville, Minn.: Liturgical Press, 1995.

Pinn, Anthony. *Why, Lord?: Suffering and Evil in Black Theology.* New York: Continuum, 1995.

Pittinger, W. Norman. "Christology in Process Theology." *Theology* 80 (May 1977): 187-93.

Plato. "Socrates' Defense (Apology)." In *The Collected Dialogues of Plato,* edited by Edith Hamilton and Huntington Cairns, 3-26. New York: Pantheon Books, 1961.

Pobee, John S., ed. *Exploring Afro-Christology.* Frankfurt am Main and New York: P. Lang, 1992.

Pöhlmann, Horst Georg. *Abriß der Dogmatik: Ein Repetitorium.* Gütersloh: Gütersloher Verlagshaus Mohn, 1973.

Porter, Stanley E., ed. *The Nature of Religious Language: A Colloquium.* Sheffield, UK: Sheffield Academic Press, 1996.

Proudfoot, Wayne. "Inquiry and the Language of the Divine." *American Journal of Theology and Philosophy* 14 (Sept. 1993): 247-55.

Quinones-Ortiz, Javier. "The Mestizo Journey: Challenges for Hispanic Theology." *Apuntes* 11 (Fall 1991): 62-72.

Raschke, Carl A. *The Alchemy of the Word: Language and the End of Theology.* Missoula, Mont.: Scholars Press, 1979.

Recinos, Harold J. *Who Comes in the Name of the Lord?: Jesus at the Margins.* Nashville: Abingdon Press, 1997.

Ringe, Sharon H. *Jesus, Liberation, and the Biblical Jubilee: Images for Ethics and Christology.* Philadelphia: Fortress Press, 1985.

Robbins, J. Wesley. "Pragmatism and the Deconstruction of Theology." *Religious Studies* 24 (Sept. 1988): 375-84.

Rockefeller, Steven C. "Pragmatism, Democracy, and God." *American Journal of Theology and Philosophy* 14 (Sept. 1993): 263-78.

Rodriguez, José David. "De 'Apuntes' a 'Esbozo': Diez Años de Reflexion." *Apuntes* 10 (Winter 1990): 75-83.

Rodríguez-Días, Daniel R. and David Cortés-Fuentes, eds. *Hidden Stories: Unveiling the History of the Latino Church.* Decatur, Ga.: Asociación para la Educación teológica Hispana, 1994.

Romaine, Suzanne. *Bilingualism.* 2nd ed. Oxford: Blackwell, 1995.

Romero, C. Gilbert. "Hispanic Theology and the Apocalyptic Imagination." *Apuntes* 15 (Winter 1995): 133-37.

———. "On Choosing a Symbol System for Hispanic Theology." *Apuntes* 1 (Winter 1981): 16-20.

Rosado, Caleb. "The Church, the City, and the Compassionate Christ." *Apuntes* 9 (Summer 1989): 27-35.

Rossing, John P. "Mestizaje and Marginality: A Hispanic American Theology." *Theology Today* 45 (Oct. 1988): 293-304.

Sanneh, Lamin O. "The Gospel, Language and Culture: The Theological Method in Cultural Analysis." *International Review of Mission* 84 (Jan.-Apr. 1995): 47-64.

Schneider, Wolfgang. "Dabar bedeudete: 's.'" *Biblische Notizen* 58 (1991): 24-28.

Schoneveld, Jocobus. "Torah in the Flesh: A New Reading of the Prologue of the Gospel of John as a Contribution to a Christology Without Anti-Judaism." *Immanuel* 24-25 (1990): 77-94.

Schori, Kurt. *Das Problem der Tradition: Eine Fundamentaltheologische Untersuchung.* Stuttgart: W. Kohlhammer, 1992.

Schulte, Andrea. *Religiöse Rede als Sprachhundlung: Eine Untersuchung ur performativen Funktion der christlichen Glaubens—und Verkündigungssprache.* Frankfurt am Main and New York: P. Lang, 1992.

Schüssler Fiorenza, Elisabeth. *Jesus: Miriam's Child, Sophia's Prophet—Critical Issues in Feminist Christology.* New York: Continuum, 1994.

———. *Searching the Scriptures, vol. 1: A Feminist Introduction.* New York: Crossroad, 1993.

Segovia, Fernando. "Aliens in the Promised Land: The Manifest Destiny of U.S. Hispanic American Theology." In *Hispanic/Latino Theology: Challenge and Promise,* edited by Ada María Isasi-Díaz and Fernando F. Segovia. Minneapolis: Fortress Press, 1996.

———. "Two Places and No Place on Which to Stand: Mixture and Otherness in Hispanic American Theology." *Listening* 27 (Winter 1992): 26-40.

———, ed. "Hispanic Americans in Theology and the Church." *Listening* 27 (Winter 1992): 3-84.

———. "A New Manifest Destiny: The Emerging Theological Voice of Hispanic Americans." *Religious Studies Review* 17 (April 1991): 102-9.

Sloyan, Gerard Stephen. *Jesus: Redeemer and Divine Word.* Wilmington, Del.: M. Glazier, 1989.

Snyder, Mary Hembrow. *The Christology of Rosemary Radford Ruether: A Critical Introduction.* Mystic, Conn.: Twenty-Third Publications, 1988.

Sobrino, Jon. *Jesus the Liberator: A Historical-Theological Reading of Jesus of Nazareth.* Translated by Paul Burns and Francis McDonagh. Maryknoll: Orbis Books, 1993.

———. *Jesus in Latin America.* Translated by Robert R. Barr. Maryknoll: Orbis Books, 1987.

———. *Christology at the Crossroads: A Latin American Approach.* Maryknoll: Orbis Books, 1978.

Soelle, Dorothee. *On Earth as in Heaven: A Liberation Spirituality of Sharing.* Translated by Marc Batko. Louisville: Westminster John Knox Press, 1993.

Solivan, Samuel. "Orthopathos: Prolegomenon for a North American Hispanic Theology." Ph.D. diss., Union Theological Seminary, N.Y., 1993.

———. "Orthopathos: Interlocutor Between Orthodoxy and Praxis." *Andover Newton Review* 1 (Winter 1990): 19-25.

Solivan-Roman, Samuel. "The Need for a North American Hispanic Theology." *Listening* 27 (Winter 1992): 17-25.

Somerville, C. John. "Is Religion a Language Game? A Real World Critique of the Cultural-Linguistic Theory." *Theology Today* 51 (Jan. 1995): 594-99.

Speyr, Adrienne von. *The Word Becomes Flesh: Meditations on John 1–5.* San Francisco: Ignatius Press, 1994.

Stevens, Maryanne, ed. *Reconstructing the Christ Symbol: Essays in Feminist Christology.* New York: Paulist Press, 1993.

Stevens-Arroyo, Antonio M. *Discovering Latino Religion: A Comprehensive Social Science Bibliography*. New York: Bildner Center for Western Hemisphere Studies, 1995.

Stevens-Arroyo, Antonio M. and Ana María Díaz-Stevens, eds. *An Enduring Flame: Studies on Latino Popular Religiosity*. New York: Bildner Center for Western Hemisphere Studies, 1994.

Stone, Bryan P. *Effective Faith: A Critical Study of the Christology of Juan Luis Segundo*. Lanham, Md.: University Press of America, 1994.

Tertullian. "Against Praxeas." In vol. 3 of *Ante-Nicene Fathers*, edited by Alexander Roberts and James Donaldson, 597-627. 2nd ed. Peabody, Mass.: Hendrickson Publishers, Inc., 1995.

Thiselton, Anthony C. "Supposed Power of Words in the Biblical Writings." *Journal of Theological Studies* 25 (Oct. 1974): 283-99.

Thompson, Marianne Meye. *The Incarnate Word: Perspectives on Jesus in the Fourth Gospel*. 2nd ed. Peabody, Mass.: Hendrickson Publishers, 1993.

Thompson, William M. *The Jesus Debate: A Survey and Synthesis*. New York: Paulist Press, 1985.

Tillich, Paul. *Theology of Culture*. Edited by Robert C. Kimball. New York: Oxford University Press, 1959.

———. *Dynamics of Faith*. New York: Harper, 1957.

———. *Systematic Theology. Vol. I: Reason and Revelation*. Chicago: University of Chicago Press, 1957.

———. *Biblical Religion and the Search for Ultimate Reality*. Chicago: University of Chicago Press, 1955.

Torres Amat, Don Felix. *La Sagrada Biblia Nuevamente Traducida al Español*. Mexico: Libreria de Galvan, 1835.

Unamuno, Miguel de. *Tragic Sense of Life*. Translated by J. E. Crawford Flitch. New York: Dover Publications, 1954.

———. *The Agony of Christianity*. Translated by Kurt F. Reinhardt. New York: F. Ungar Publishing Co., 1960.

———. "Spanish Religion." In *The English Woman* 4 (Dec. 1909).

Van der Watt, Jan G. "The Composition of the Prologue of John's Gospel: The Historical Jesus Introducing Divine Grace." *Westminster Theological Journal* 57 (Fall 1995): 311-32.

Van Ness, Peter H. "Linguistic Self-Reference and Religious Language." *Union Seminary Quarterly Review* 41 (1987): 1-12.

Von Balthasar, Hans Urs. *A Theology of History*. 2nd ed. New York: Sheed & Ward, 1963.

Vorster, Johannes. "Creatures Creating Creators: The Potential of Rhetoric." *Religion and Theology* 1 (1994): 118-35.

Wallace, Darryl K. "Jesus Ain't Got No Feet: A Black Perspective on Christology." *Urban Mission* 6 (Jan. 1989): 13-23.

Waltermire, Donald E. *The Liberation Christologies of Leonardo Boff and Jon Sobrino: Latin American Contributions to Contemporary Christology*. Lanham, Md.: University Press of America, 1994.

Ward, Graham. *Barth, Derrida and the Language of Theology*. Cambridge and New York: Cambridge University Press, 1995.

Weddle, David L. "The Liberator as Exorcist: James Cone and the Classic Doctrine of Atonement." *Religion in Life* 49 (Winter 1980): 477-87.

Wells, Harold. "Trinitarian Feminism: Elizabeth Johnson's Wisdom Christology." *Theology Today* 52 (Oct. 1995): 330-43.

Whitehead, Alfred North. *Process and Reality: An Essay in Cosmology.* Corrected ed. New York: Free Press, 1978.

———. *Modes of Thought.* New York: Macmillan, 1938.

Williamson, Ronald. "The Incarnation of the Logos in Hebrews." *Expository Times* 95 (Oct. 1983): 4-8.

Wilmore, Gayraud S., ed. *African American Religious Studies: An Interdisciplinary Anthology.* Durham, N.C.: Duke University Press, 1989.

———. "Black Messiah: Revising the Color Symbolism of Western Christology." *Journal of the Interdenominational Theological Center* 2 (Fall 1974): 8-18.

Winquist, Charles E. "Metaphor and the Accession to Theological Language." *Journal of the American Academy of Religion Thematic Studies* 49 (1982): 73-84.

Wittgenstein, Ludwig. *On Certainty.* Edited by G. E. M. Anscombe and G. H. von Wright. Translated by Denis Paul and G. E. M. Anscombe. Oxford: Blackwell, 1969.

———. *Lectures and Conversations: On Aesthetics, Psychology, and Religious Belief.* Edited by Cyril Barrett. Berkeley: University of California Press, 1967.

———. *Preliminary Studies for "Philosophical Investigations," Generally Known as the Blue and Brown Books.* New York: Harper & Row, 1965.

———. *Philosophical Investigations.* 2nd ed. Translated by G. E. M. Anscombe. New York: Macmillan, 1958.

Wolterstorff, Nicholas. *Divine Discourse: Philosophical Reflections on the Claim That God Speaks.* Cambridge and New York: Cambridge University Press, 1995.

Wondra, Ellen K. *Humanity Has Been a Holy Thing: Toward a Contemporary Feminist Christology.* Lanham, Md.: University Press of America, 1994.

Wong, Joseph H. P. *Logos-Symbol in the Christology of Karl Rahner.* Rome: LAS, 1984.

Young, Pamela Dickey. "Diversity in Feminist Christology." *Studies in Religion* 21 (1992): 81-90.

Youngman, Nilah M. "Affirming Hispanic Women." Ph.D. diss., Austin Presbyterian Theological Seminary, 1993.

Zambrano, Ariel. "Content and Context of Evangelization: An Hispanic Perspective." Ph.D. diss., School of Theology at Claremont, 1986.